Introduction

There has existed for some time an unfortunate discrepancy in art education between literature which deals with the elementary art program and that which concerns itself with the secondary schools – with most writing concentrating in the elementary level. The art of the child admittedly has had a certain mystique going for it – not the least of which is the engaging nature of childhood itself. Because of the rapid changes of development in learning and in physical growth, the art of the child has captured the attention of psychologists, educators, and artists since the turn of the century. The art of the emerging adult has, unfortunately, not enjoyed equal attention – any more than one's 16-year-old gets the same kind of loving attention as his 6-year-old sibling. The record shows that most of the writers who have the greatest influence on art educators (Viktor Lowenfeld, Sir Herbert Read, June King McFee, etc.) have developed their theories from the vantage point of the child rather than the adolescent.

John Portchmouth's book, therefore, fulfills a real need, as it provides fresh insight into the problem of getting teenagers involved in the visual arts. The fact that his experiments are drawn from British schools makes them no less relevant to the American experience. Portchmouth's book is not a scholarly work, nor will a teacher turn to it for a carefully researched body of theory. (Art teachers, for the most part, are not apt to seek out such books in any case.) What this book does offer is a record of how one capable teacher goes about his job with a clear eye for the practical workaday problems at hand. All teaching is a matter of prediction, and the author obviously has the experience to know pretty well the many causal relationships which can exist in the teaching situation. He has a particular sensitivity to the sources of art, to the many worlds of motivation, as well as to the kinds of problems which can 'grab' a youngster. Portchmouth opts for a wide gamut of experience and deals tellingly with the polarities of observation and imagination, and like most art teachers, he is particularly aware of the role of media as a potential source of art activity. He also places quite a premium upon the role art can play in general education and has many suggestions for getting art out of the studio and into the rooms of his colleagues.

Like all good teachers he has an affinity for the gut level – the 'affect,' if you will – of the situation. His own personal regard for the task of teaching lends a warm patina of affection which illuminates the text. *Secondary School Art* is for those who are capable of recognizing and responding to this.

AL HURWITZ, Coordinator of Arts
Newton Public Schools, Newton, Massachusetts

Secondary School Art

John Portchmouth

VAN NOSTRAND REINHOLD COMPANY

NEW YORK   CINCINNATI   TORONTO   LONDON   MELBOURNE

To my family

N
350
P6
1971

Acknowledgments
The work illustrated in the book is from the following schools, and
the author wishes to thank all the students and teachers concerned:
Bedminster Down School, Bristol; Clifton Hight School for Girls, Bristol;
Cotham Boys' Grammar School, Bristol; County Hight School, Coal-
brookdale; Duncan Bowen Secondary School, Ashford; Gillingham
School, Dorset; Heron Wood County Secondary School, Aldershor;
Hugh Clopton Secondary School for Boys, Stratford; Kilburn Senior
High School, London; Kingsfield School, Kingswood; Oldborough
Manor County Secondary School, Maidstone; Parliament Hill School,
London; Sidcot School, Somerset; Technical High School for Girls,
Maidstone; Westlands Secondary School, Sittingbourne; Westwing
School, Thornbury; Wingham School, Canterbury.

Photography by the staff of the schools, Ronald P. Meyer and the author.

Van Nostrand Reinhold Company Regional Offices:
New York   Cincinnati   Chicago   Milbrae   Dallas

Van Nostrand Reinhold Company International Offices:
London   Toronto   Melbourne

Photoset and printed by
BAS Printers Ltd, Wallop, Hampshire, England
First published in England by Studio Vista
Blue Star House, Highgate Hill, London N19
Published in the U.S.A by
Van Nostrand Reinhold Company
A Division of Litton Educational Publishing, Inc.
450 West 33rd Street, New York, N.Y. 10001

Contents

1 Why do we teach art in secondary schools?

In a discussion recently among student-teachers someone asked, 'Why do we teach art since surely it is a natural gift? Some people are born with it and some are not – and either way it is what you want to express yourself, not what others can teach you.' It may help us to answer this by deciding first what we mean by 'teaching art'. We would probably all agree that the ability to draw and paint and use other materials expressively is indeed a gift, just as writing and singing are, and that like other gifts it is natural to most young children. The nature of the gift will vary with the child, but it can develop under fair conditions or fall into neglect under less happy ones: it needs the right conditions in order to grow. These conditions are found first of all in the home with the help and opportunities that the child finds there. They are also found in the art environment at school, where the exchange of ideas and experiments is taking place all the time. The teacher who provides the right kind of opportunities and materials has set the scene: as he discovers the best way to give everyone confidence in using them, he is teaching art. The student needs a chance to work things out for himself, and reassurance or assistance when he cannot; he needs materials and ideas with which to manoeuvre. The teacher is there to supply them.

A further question was raised, 'Why do we go on teaching art at secondary level when so many students seem to have lost interest by this age and when they also have to concentrate on other examination subjects?' I think it should be said first of all that undoubtedly some students *do* lose interest in art, and that neither they nor the teacher should be in the position of having to continue in the face of total lack of interest. But these instances are far fewer than would at first appear, especially if the teacher has time to get to know his students better and can discover what they feel to be important and worth expressing.

If, earlier on, a youngster has found in his drawings and paintings a way of dealing with the simpler world of childhood, it is certain that he will need them still more in the difficult world of adolescence. There is more to sort out, more to understand and enjoy, more that angers. And at this time too, he can begin to see further possibilities for experiment with materials, and he is ready to start using them. Because he can now express himself through other means, like writing, speaking, acting, and making music, and is finding other studies absorbing, it does not follow that he has nothing to say through art. There will always be experiences that can only really happen with colour and line and form: and if these dry up for him, where does he turn?

The argument went on: 'Does he have the *time* now for art?

Should he have to worry about it when he has to put so much into his main courses?' Any subject, taught as a live experience, keeps initiative and discovery alive, and therefore any discipline can be expressive. But, by their nature, academic or theoretical studies develop largely within a predictable and agreed framework. The student should still be able to follow up his own, more personal, responses. As long as he can continue to express these with paints and clay and wood and any other materials he can find, he should be able to do so.

'But,' someone insisted, 'what are we really trying to do? Are we trying to make artists of as many youngsters as we can, or are we just using art to help them to be well-balanced personalities?' By trying to develop a child's expressive ability, however slight this may be, the teacher is persuading him to make fuller use of it, bringing out the artist in him and, at the same time, educating him as a person. The child's skills in art are not something apart from his other learning and experience: they only make sense together. How far a student will take his art depends on what it has meant to him right through his childhood and adolescence. If it has been important, he may go into it more deeply in his later years, and the teacher should encourage him as in any other field. His ideas will have led him to experiment in different ways and any success will suggest the areas in which he can be helped. So, in a way, the teacher is doing all the things mentioned: he is educating the students to be the artists and the personalities they are, and he is equipping them to venture as far as their interests take them.

More and more teaching is taking place in areas of sprawling urban development which lack the stimulus of either town and city life, or of the countryside. How can teaching meet the very special needs of adolescents who spend their whole lives here? Much of beauty and value can be found even in these areas by drawing on the deep human interests and relationships involved; but art teaching should be ready to attack – and attack hard – all forms of ugliness and dullness that such surroundings breed. The teacher has to prevent his students from slipping into a weary acceptance of their environment and its synthetic trappings by directing them again and again to the great natural materials of the world – by introducing these materials into the classroom, by taking the classes out, by encouraging their own wider searches: he will need to take them to places of character, to fine buildings and into situations where creative work is going on. He has little to assist him (books and films and talking will only go so far) and his job is probably harder than in schools more happily situated. His efforts will concentrate on making art a time and a place for protest (rather than resignation), for spirited adventure (rather than weary pursuits), and for joy in a young world (not dejection among the stale patterns of an old). This book looks further at how it can be done, remembering that each teacher must decide for himself the best way in the end. Only *he* is in a position to know the lives concerned.

2 The new arrivals – a changing art

Long before a youngster comes to his secondary school, his art has been taking shape and will already have passed through changes that both checked and elated him. At a very early age he found that he could say things about himself and what happened to him by making pictures of them. He may have found he could use other materials like clay and wood and scrap of various kinds to do this: a twisted root and nails became a dragon; three cardboard boxes could be changed into a house. He turned them into like-nesses of what he knew and felt about life. What he made had the instant rightness that he imagined for it, much as the broom handle was a horse the moment he was astride. His means were simply anything that was around and seemed suitable, anything that would

Fig. 1 The world they have left

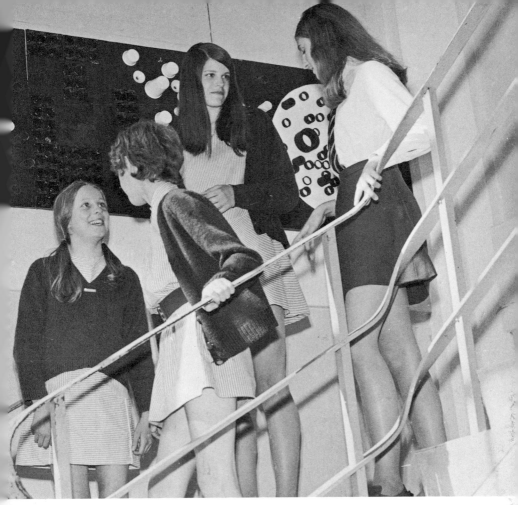

Fig. 2 The world they have joined

make a mark or that he could shape or put together quickly. By these means he felt his way into the circumstances and conditions in which he grew up, projecting his sense of his own body and movement, his innermost thoughts and feelings, into a form that he could see. What was important was doing it: imagination was to make up for any shortcomings in the result. His first inventions, particularly in drawing and painting, led him over the years to arrive at certain ways of representing his commonest experiences: himself, other people, animals, trees, houses, vehicles, all began to take on fixed shapes in his work by which they could be recognized. He built up a pictorial language of symbols, strangely like that of most other children of his age, and he could use this range of symbols, with only slight variations here and there, to express anything he wanted to, either actual or imaginary. The experience itself and representing it were equally real: and reality was a game of hide-and-seek between fact and imagination.

It is not easy for an adult to look back into that childhood world, but we can wonder at those bold, unprecedented statements that seem so close to the sense or thought for which they stood. A child can put it down so clearly – to his own satisfaction anyway. Then the position begins to get more complicated. The world fills out with forms and colours and surfaces, changing all the time under the effects of light and movement. Feelings and sensations become difficult to account for. Ideas are many-sided. People behave unpredictably. He is looking at the past and the future with different eyes. The symbols he used before for what he knew of life are not equal to its growing scale, and each time he tries to use them, they are less so. Those that were all right a short while ago are not so now; ones that are all right today will be wrong tomorrow or the next day. Also, he is beginning to find unexpected interpretations for what he has drawn or made. Often he is influenced by the interpretations other people put on it and he comes less and less to be able to depend on his symbols, as events compel him to consider them more critically. About the same time, other changes are taking place. Where crayons and paints had given him a way of putting down all that happened, more and more new words are appearing to help him talk and write about it. Where a piece of wood or a can or a sea-shell had become what he made it, he is learning the secrets of what they really are. And at some point, the magic of counting opens up before him. With each age, there are new discoveries and inventions: words, magnifying glasses, measuring tools, all come within reach, and he begins to let his crayons and brushes go. Experience introduces him to other ways of thinking, other ways of saying things.

There may be the eleven-year-old who is still able to express the meaning of the moment or thought with just the right material and tool. He may be able to meet each change with a confident change in his work as new knowledge directs it; but it is more likely that he will not be able to do this. His experience will have out-run his ability to interpret it, and response and expression will have drifted apart.

Something else will also have been happening almost unnoticed over the years since he first began to splash colours on to paper. This has to do with the way he uses the paint. As a young child, he started by simply enjoying the coloured marks it made. Later on, when he was a little older, he wanted to make the marks mean something, and he found that he had to put the paint on in a certain way to obtain these effects. When he had done so and looked at the result, he remembered how he did it, and the next time he made a picture he repeated the process in much the same fashion. Gradually over a period his brush and paint came to retrace the motions and effects of preceding experiences. He was developing a particular manner of applying the paint, each attempt a little more like the one before. Yet all the while this was going on, his expressive *needs* were changing. They were different from the ones that first produced the painting process earlier on, a process no longer developing fresh impetus from each new *reason* for painting. New experiences made him want to paint them, but the manner of painting remained the same, following habits already formed. The picture he really wanted did not come, and it ended up much the same as any of its predecessors, or just became something that was not important to him. Expression was limited to the level at which his technique settled down.

What happened with paint may also have happened with other materials he used consistently, such as clay; though these would be unlikely to have had the same place in his experience as painting.

He may only now, however, be aware of the changes that have been overtaking him, and of the limit of the resources left to him. Does he know where things went wrong; why he cannot say what he really wants to; why the important things have to be passed over because they take him beyond the marks and forms he knows how to make? Does he wonder why the areas in which he *can* do something are getting fewer − areas secure for a little longer in childhood because no new knowledge has challenged them? 'The witch' may be as innocently sinister as ever; and 'Caverns under the sea' may still be the exotic gardens and zoos they once were. For the rest − the present and real happenings, the effects he is trying to achieve − he has to make do by altering the old symbols, by bending lines and padding out shapes and by a new detail tacked on here and there. His attempts suffer further from comparison with the realistic work he sees around him everywhere in illustrations, photographs, reproductions, and the work of older people.

Although this probably all began back in his primary days, its effects may only now be starting to appear. They can be seen in several ways:

1 A gradual withdrawal from any really personal attempt at expression.
2 Recourse to copying or to 'shorthand' art forms picked up from caricatures and cartoons.
3 The use of rulers and compasses to help him draw.
4 A return to earlier symbols − becoming, at this later stage, stiff and lifeless from inert repetition.
5 Retreat into pattern making − secure from the kind of criticism levelled at his more natural efforts.
6 Leaving work unfinished where his symbols let him down.

13

If only he had not come to believe – or others had not persuaded him – that the things he created when he was three were infantile, instead of contemporary and right! If only the things he had made at six had not been dismissed as childish, and he had not copied others so much to improve them! If only what he did at nine had not been received with amusement and superior airs as only the poor attempts of youth, instead of the achievements of youth, he would not have strained so hard to better them with more sophisticated ones drawn from elsewhere and looking like a thousand others, but not like *his*! The mine is closing over, and it is not so easy to bring its treasures to the surface.

Would it have been any different if the young environment had been filled with more materials and tools and the time to use them? I knew a boy once who made a maze of nails hammered into a piece of old floorboard; he stretched and tightened thread across them into a mesh because he had had a nightmare in which someone was shutting him in just like that. Afterwards, he plucked at the threads and made dull notes. He listened to them and a new sense seemed to take over from the old idea. He started again with another piece of wood, more nails, and fine wire this time – and he made it so that he could play better notes, unusual and faintly oriental (fig. 3). But we all liked it. Then he made up some words about being lost in a labyrinth and finding his way out by standing still till the exit came to *him*. But then he was lucky: he was allowed to work out his nightmare and his notes and his fable; he was not

Fig. 3 The labyrinth

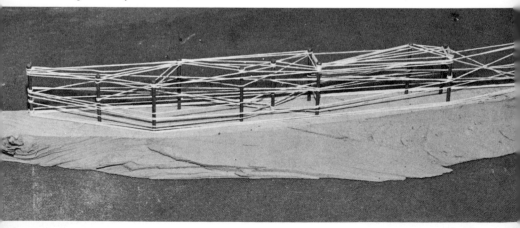

called suddenly to get down to something else that was thought more important. If he had been, he would have been left with his nightmare and the comfort of page 3 algebra and four dates in the history of the Anglo-Saxons to reassure him: by page 4 and the fifth date, the half-remembered labyrinth would have sunk beyond recall and would have lain a wreck and a danger beneath his future ways. But that was only one boy. Even he was probably caught up in the drift away from confident expression, as another student might be now – a student in front of us in our own class.

It is clear that around the age when the move from primary to secondary school takes place, spoken language is naturally expanding from day to day to keep pace with experience as it happens. But the same is not true where art is concerned. The adolescent can not turn to it at any moment as he can to words and say what is in his mind. So it falls more and more behind the moment for which it was meant; and when he *can* use it, so much has happened since that it is not worth saying any longer. So he says something less important, and with means that are out-of-date. The student needs help across these lengthening intervals so that he can continue to say *what* matters *when* it matters, or as near the event as possible. He needs help in finding means to express himself in his own advancing world – finding, in a way, a new visual language that he can then go on renewing. Without this help, he can so easily abandon the attempt and put aside a dimension of experience that might otherwise have remained open. What is unexpressed when the need is greatest is likely to stay so: he will have moved forward and beyond it without the achievement or understanding it could have given him.

The problem and the solution are both clear if we look at this question of words. We take it for granted that a growing child will talk endlessly and use words almost non-stop in an attempt to say what he wants to about the way he feels and what he is thinking and doing. He is experimenting all the while, getting through millions of words to find the ones that work best. We accept this incredible 'wastage': it is part of the never-ending business of learning what one wants to say and how to make oneself understood. It is not until he has been doing this for several years that he begins to manage words confidently and well. Do we accept this 'wastage' in drawings and paintings? Can we see that a child will have to make as many drawings and paintings before he can begin to feel the same confidence and express himself as clearly? There will be countless beginnings, countless failures, before it can happen. Are we too eager that every time he puts crayon or brush to paper he should produce something intelligible? Do we look for too much from each attempt, expecting it to show an improvement on the last? Does the child begin to expect this of himself as well because he senses our expectations? The adolescent learns to expect it even more.

Word-making comes about so very gradually: writing grows through imperceptibly small advances. Can picture-making grow any faster? It is so easy to come up behind a picture and suggest what could be done to make it better. The student may have been at grips with only a fragment of experience or a passing thought. It means no more than a little gush of words would do. Its job is done. There is nothing more than that in it. Soon it will happen again with a different thought. It was not meant to be anything special, or to be laboured at until it was complete. A well-expressed sentence is not made by hammering away at the arrangement of words: a lot of speaking and writing has to go on first. A well-expressed picture is not made by hammering at it, by correcting 'mistakes', by trying to get it perfect every time; but all too often, this is exactly what takes place. If pictures and other forms of visual expression are to develop as naturally as speech, we must be prepared for most of them to be over and done with just as quickly. They have happened: that is enough. They may never come to light again. By far the greatest part of all that is produced – certainly the most formative – is of this kind.

The step that boys and girls take from the primary school to the secondary school is a short one in time but a big one in their own history. This is a world of different proportions and different prospects. The students are the youngest ones, where, in their last school, they were the oldest. Everywhere there are signs and talk of what is ahead. Subjects they know about look as though they are going to be more difficult: subjects they have not yet met are about to break in on them. And somewhere in this scene is the art room.

To have a special room for art may be undreamed of for some. Everything looks too big, and half the things a mystery: across the tables, glimpses of nameless equipment and strange tools; and in cupboards, such materials as they have never seen. Already they will be wondering what they will be doing here, what it will be like. Some are sure of themselves and can hardly wait to begin: they have always liked art, and people have liked what they did, and now they are going to do more of it – only better. Some are not quite as sure, and view the prospect with a vague uneasiness. The rest feel sure that they cannot do art at all, never have been able to, and never will. For them, the room is an empty space, and nothing will happen for them there – not that they can look forward to, at least. At the centre of all this is the art teacher. He (or she) may be the first 'artist' they have met, and they will be divided, according to their feelings, between a frenzy to show him what they can do and a grave reluctance to do so. Either way they will be asking themselves what he will think of them and what he will expect of them. For many, this is the first time in their lives they are really in the art world, despite any lively scenes they may have lived through in their primary days. This has all the feel of the real thing!

Many secondary schools do not have a special art room, and make do with an ordinary classroom adapted for the purpose when art comes round. Temporary rearrangement of desks and tables, the sudden appearance of paints and brushes and other materials, and the ceremonial opening of a particular cupboard, may be the only token that a change has taken place and that any signs of a previous mathematics or geography lesson can be ignored. But even here it can be felt as something of a special occasion. However, the way events are going to work out for the students will depend not so much on the room and the facilities as on the teacher and the kind of feeling he is going to create among them. It will depend too on the way they influence each other. How will they all get on together?

Look at them a moment. Boys . . . girls . . . growing out of their jackets and skirts . . . growing through them . . . getting bigger while we watch . . . quiet, noisy, neglected, indulged, timid, bold, surly, savage, idle, sensitive, resigned – all of them from different homes, different families, different things happening to them or about to happen, things they think about, feel about, feel nothing about, wish they were doing – all different. How can we believe that at this moment or any moment they are all going to be interested in the same thing, or that they will get much from it? Do we know what each of them would try to say if he could, what they have not been able to say so far: the secrets, the pleasant thoughts and the terrible thoughts, the waiting for something, the hurt they cannot understand or deal with, the thing that thrills or deeply disturbs? They cannot talk about it (that is why it may *be* important). Can they do so in a picture or a model? It would not matter if it slipped away again afterwards: at least they would have seen it a little more clearly. They are nearer to their vision than they think. How can we reach them so that what they do makes them glad, makes them laugh or feel relieved? There are so many of them – so much talking – so many attitudes and tempers, open and veiled! They are all in it together: there is no place for remembering what is important –

only what is on the surface, the clear-as-daylight, hard-as-desktop kind of remembering. They are so often drawn into little objectives with advantages that last as long as a handful of sea brought back to a sand hole: things their eyes and hands do that leave their lives outside: mirrors we hold up for them to see the obvious in. They have to go along with it – everyone does. Where there is no real need, the material will say nothing . . . attractive patterns, pictures that are well worked out, clever models, yes: but the private worlds will be driven further below the surface, private searches abandoned, private discoveries covered over because they are not like everything else being done. No one must think about it too much, but just get on and do it.

Every teacher knows how difficult the position is, and that he has to do what he can with the time and opportunities before him. His own clear thinking will be behind whatever compromise he has to make with an uncompromising situation.

3   Thinking about the lessons

Whose ideas?
Can I, for a moment, set the scene in an imaginary art room, let the characters talk, and then try to do what I have already suggested is impossible – look into the thoughts of an adolescent in the class, following them in words that must unavoidably be my own?

'Peter! – quiet everyone! Peter! Now what was I saying? Quiet at
   the back! What was I saying, Peter?'
'You asked what we passed on the way to school.'
'I said that five minutes ago. What was the last thing I said?'
'He was showing me his paper, sir.'
'You just haven't been listening, have you! Have you!'
'Yes, sir.'
'Five minutes ago!'
'He was showing me his paper, sir.'
'What's that got to do with it? I was talking to you. What were
   you doing looking at papers?'
'He showed it to me, sir.'
'Aren't you interested in what we're going to do?'
'Can we draw an aeroplane, sir?'
'I asked you a question. Are you interested in what we're doing?'
'Is it aeroplanes, sir?'
'Did you see one on your way to school?'
'I did once, sir. Can I draw it?'
'Let's wait and see. Now listen again everyone. Peter! Come here.
   What's the matter with you – you're talking again . . .'

. . . coming to school . . . what did I see . . . what does it matter
. . . why does he want to know? I don't remember . . . can't see
that it matters . . . broke a cup this morning and shoved it in the
dustbin – ought to have stuffed it right down under the papers –
I'll get bawled at when I get home . . . what did I see on the way to
school . . . dad left for work without saying anything . . . what did
I see . . . football after break – left my shorts under the bed – I
hate football . . . on the way to school . . . looking over a new bike
tomorrow – wait till I get it: I'll show Sid who's got the best one –
he might bash it – he's bigger than me – wish I was bigger . . . what
does it matter what I saw coming to school? We weren't run over,
were we! We saw all the cars and buses, didn't we! And got here
all right! We saw all we needed to . . .

What is uppermost in his thoughts and responses?
He may be falling back on the only thing he knows how to draw (an
aeroplane), or he may really want to do it; he may have other things

in mind and will need only a little encouragement to attempt them. Other students may have thought of something they would like to make together. And then there will be those who look entirely to the teacher for ideas and direction. Whichever is the case, they will all need time and a chance to sort out their ideas. Any lesson should allow for one or all of these to happen. It is worth spending a little time looking at these different approaches in detail:

1 *The student who comes with an idea of his own and wants to carry it out.*

In this case, the fact that the idea is important to him will probably mean that he can start work right away without much help. He may have gone as far as collecting his own materials, and it is worth encouraging this, even though what he brings may not be entirely suitable and have to be reconsidered in the light of his plans. It is more probable, however, that he will hope to find materials from those in the art room.

He must be clear about his responsibility for any materials or tools he takes. The teacher will know a safe range to make available. Certain tools are obviously dangerous if used without guidance or supervision; but even a limited range can cover most needs: if not, it will mean that the student has to modify his approach or improvise other means. The result could well turn out to be closer to his own ideas.

The teacher must guess from his knowledge of the student how well he is able to carry out his intention, and will be guided by the direction it takes. He will notice how long it is sustained, where it begins to break down, and why. The help he gives will depend on what happens. An idea that the student wants to work out for himself is, after all, the kind that really matters: and art teaching must aim for this as much as possible.

The boy in fig. 4 came to the lesson with the firm idea of making a large bird sculpture to erect outside his aviary at home. He brought along some materials and found the rest from among the store of scrap pieces in the art room. He experimented with ways of assembling and supporting the form he wanted (an osprey with its catch) and put it all together with very little help from the teacher. He drilled and fixed the main parts and completed the modelling with net-curtaining soaked in plaster, giving it a metallic finish for protection. The teacher can learn more about a student in a situation like this than he can from one he has devised himself.

A student working alone is still one of the class and should fit in without disturbing it, but he should be reasonably free of any overall direction that the lesson takes for others.

Fig. 4 Boy aged 13

Fig. 5 Boys aged 12

Fig. 6 Boys aged 15

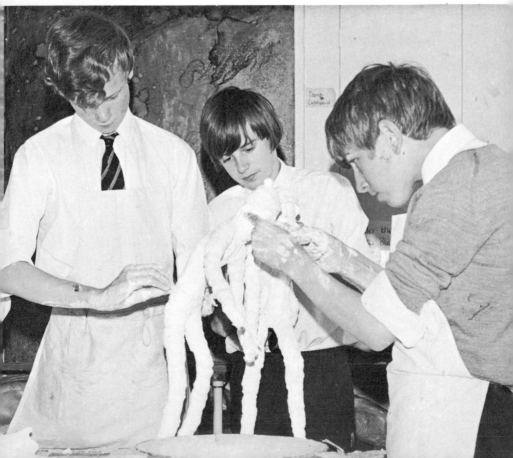

Fig. 7 The finished work

2 *A number of students who come with an idea of their own and want to carry it out together.*

The students have discovered an interest among themselves and agreed on how it can be worked out, perhaps even to the extent of finding materials and deciding what each is going to do. Again, the teacher must consider the value of the project for the group and come in on the selection of materials and tools where necessary. The combined ideas and abilities of the group may be sufficient to carry the job through on their own, and though one or two may take the lead, the initiative will remain with the group as a whole, working together to the end they have in mind. Their influence on each other will decide the course of events, and this can be more constructive than the influence of an older person who may not have entered fully into their plans. There will clearly be times, however, when the teacher will be able to help the group sort out their ideas. As with a student working alone, they are still part of the class and will fit into its wider organization.

In the illustrations, students are shown working together on

23

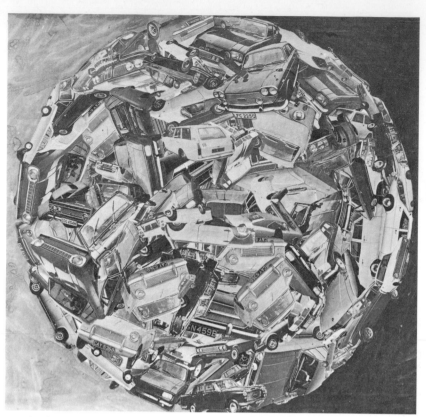
Fig. 8 Boys aged 14/15

constructions they have planned between them. In fig. 5 they are using balsa wood strips to see how large and complex a structure they can build with them. In fig. 6 two other students are modelling plaster onto an armature of wood and metal. They share all stages of the work – making the armature, preparing the plaster and scrim, building up the forms, and finishing off (fig. 7). Fig. 8 is the work of four students who had thought up the idea themselves and brought along a few magazines from which to cut out the pictures of cars they needed (more magazines had to be found later). The collage conveys the congestion of town traffic – with obvious undertones of the scrap heap! The students' own experience and personal comment are both present.

3 *Students who come with no ideas of their own and look to the teacher to provide them.*
The teacher presents an idea or a subject for the students to explore and develops the lesson from this.

It should be said here that the directed lesson can become a habit and assume too easily that the class have no ideas of their own. A lesson that over-rides private questioning and needs is about as far removed from the creative situation as it is possible to be. It can only throw impediments across the paths of those concerned, or lay false trails to meaningless ends. The one occasion in the week when students could have found help in saying something that, matters to them, is taken up in dealing with things that do not matter and about which they feel nothing.

In general, **the presented lesson should only be for those who need it and can do nothing without it**. How many in the class this represents will depend on the confidence the students have learned in developing their own ideas. This is not just a matter of the teacher's influence but of personal backgrounds and relationships. Some students can find real stimulus from an idea presented to them, and discover attitudes of their own in interpreting it: pressures and confusions in their lives may be too great for them to find a single focus by themselves, or they may be in a wilderness and glad of a signpost; or they may just not care. There could be other reasons why the teacher's classes depend on him more than he would wish. He is working within an educational and social situation that unfortunately has this effect, and at the same time limits what he can do about it. The sheer numbers in his class, the syllabus-ridden structure of the schools, the academic weight of courses, attitudes rooted in conventions of art and art teaching – all are against his carrying out experiments in creative learning. The most he can hope for in these circumstances is to plan within a longer-term perspective of his students' lives as far as he understands them, and keep to the realities and fantasies that cluster there. He must try to make each lesson connect in some way with earlier experiences and lead on towards new ones. He can only provide the situation: its ultimate value lies in what the student makes of it.

Materials and tools

Materials are the resources that are organized and given a new shape in the creative act. Tools are the means by which this is done. There are two kinds of material and tool – natural ones and manufactured ones. Natural materials are those that are used in their natural state: stone, wood, garden clay, chalk, leaves, fleece, straw, feathers, pigments from natural sources like plants and earths. In the same way, natural tools are what they imply: slivers of wood used as paint spreaders, shells used as modelling or printmaking tools, and the hands of course. Manufactured materials are those that have been prepared or made up: paper, metal, glass, building block, plastic, paints, fabric, hardboard (U.S. masonite). Similarly with manufactured tools: hammers, chisels, knives, brushes, scissors. Some natural materials have been processed: pottery clay, wool, roof slate, cane.

The teacher has to decide on a selection of materials and tools for his own classes. He will probably include at least a few that are familiar to them. Any links with earlier days carry a sense of continuity and help the student to connect with his present opportunities. If a student has had an enjoyable experience with a medium, he will be glad to find it again in the new school and be able to continue with it. If the experience was not encouraging, he may be anxious to avoid it unless the teacher can help him find a fresh approach. The student's experience of powder paint, for example, may have been limited to certain colours, and a greater choice, with the further excitement of mixing, may give him a new feeling for it; he may not have realized he could produce such rich and delicate effects. Alternatively, he may have thought of a medium mainly in connection with a certain kind of work, e.g. balsa wood to assemble airframe kits, fabric scraps to dress a puppet. In each case the student may be surprised to discover other ways in which they can be used. A further stimulus will lie in the variety of work in these and other media that he sees going on around him.

Thoughts that might affect a teacher's reason for including a particular medium could be: Would it be likely to appeal to the students? Would they be able to manage it expressively? Have I (the teacher) any experience in working with it? If not, could I safely include it if I can see its value for certain students? With only limited experience, could I help a student to explore it fully? Is the room equipped and big enough for it? Could I manage a group working with it? Does it contribute to the all-round experience in the courses? Is there time to develop it in a worthwhile way?

Of course, most teachers would not have to catalogue questions in this way. As they get to know their classes they soon equip the room with a balanced variety of materials. One of the questions, however, may repay a closer look: 'Have I (the teacher) experience in working with a certain material?'

It is inevitable that from time to time there will be materials that the teacher has not used himself. While he should have at least some knowledge of how a material behaves before offering it to the class, a limited knowledge could prevent him seeing its possibilities, setting an unintentional limit to what the student attempts with it. The teacher need not, however, let his inexperience worry him too much. The younger mind will have less restraint and will tackle it with a freshness an older person would find difficult. On the other hand, the value of the teacher's own skills should not be underplayed: to teach away from them for the sake of mere spread is to overlook those areas where he can best extend the students, and where his own craft conviction would probably come through strongly.

It is not always possible to anticipate the moment for bringing new materials into use. If a variety of materials and tools forms part of the environment, they will attract interest and speculation either way, and this is an opportunity for the teacher. Only a few students may be involved at first, but once they have started, the effect could snowball and others be drawn into it. The teacher could then introduce the material to the class as a whole, discussing its nature and giving guidance as the work proceeds. Should such an interest overtake work that a student is already doing, the teacher will have to decide whether the change-over is likely to extend the previous work, or at least lead in a profitable direction. If not, he may encourage the student to finish what he was doing before going on to something new. However, he *could* be holding a student back: the moment may be just right for a change and could pass if the earlier work were resumed reluctantly. The use of one medium could at any time lead into another quite naturally; but there may be other occasions when the teacher wishes to move the whole class towards a new experience with materials, or to demonstrate a process clearly to avoid mishap or wastage, or where considerable disappointment would result otherwise. He will have the room and the things he needs ready for this, and he must introduce it in the way that he feels fits best into what the class has been doing up till then.

Let us now look at a few mistaken assumptions. First, that there are certain materials suitable for girls and others for boys and that sex separates exclusive needs. In fact, girls may manage wood or wire or stone as expressively as boys, and boys may do the same with fabric, threads or modelled paper. What they make of them may be different, but the materials have their own special value for both. Second, that any single material can be expected to appeal to everyone in the class as a means of dealing with a given subject, or because it fits into a planned 'programme' of activities. It is most unlikely that this would ever be the case. Third, that a medium which the teacher himself is familiar with is necessarily easy for those using it for the first time, or even that he can teach it best. Clay that forms effortlessly for a pottery-trained teacher may be only a sticky mess and quite distasteful to a student; fabric and sequins that assemble like magic for a teacher in embroidery may mean nothing to a student preoccupied with sculptural forms.

The first experience with a material is always a fresh one, and anything done with it is a discovery. With repeated use, responses become overlaid with attitudes towards it and make for self-criticism. This is inevitable, and just as it can lead to inhibition or dull repetitiveness, so on the other hand it is the only way to

Fig 9
a Boy aged 13

b First attempt at wood carving

achieving confident expression. A young student coming to his first block of wood with a few simple tools will set about carving without wondering too much what will happen and what he should or should not be doing (fig. 9b). All his attention goes into making a shape of some kind – a shape he has seen in it, or one he finds as he goes along. But the important thing is that each cut is a discovery – a surprise about what the tool does, and how the effects can be used. The chances are that he will be quite pleased with the result: he enjoys doing it because he is not worried about what it *should* look like. He is a little astonished how far he has been able to bring it from the original shape of the block; and he is probably not in a position to compare it with other carvings. This stage will pass however. He will approach each carving with more knowledge and be more critical of what happens. But he can still go on making discoveries. Every encounter with wood is different; his ideas and imagination are changing, showing him new things in it; he is learning by degrees what he can do with the tools. The progression from response to expression is constantly renewed as he feels more into the nature of the material and the forms it can develop. For another student, there will be other forms. The wood will have its own associations and suggest other possibilities. What he makes of it will depend on how he reacts and how he uses the tools.

If this is true for wood and gouges, it is also true for paint and brushes, for stone and chisels, for fabric and dyes, for clay and chalk and metal and all other materials open to experiment. Attitudes develop from a relationship with the material, both physically (in the way it is seen and felt and behaves) and imaginatively (in the way it takes shape), Fig. 10.

A material has all the possibilities within the limits to which it can be worked, and in keeping with its character. A block of plaster and a block of salt are both brittle, but their composition affects the nature of this brittleness; one has a dull whiteness, the other a glittering whiteness; one has resistance to moisture, the other has not; the texture of one allows detail carving, the texture of the other only broad carving; one can be combined with other materials, the other less so. The characteristics of all materials – their weight, composition, texture, colour, transparency, flexibility, resonance, personal associations – all affect the student's response and their value for him. In the same way, a tool has all the versatility he finds for it; and apart from any special purpose it has, he can put it to any use. The possibilities of either the material or the tool cannot be guessed from what others have achieved with them. There is no way of knowing what impact they will have on a student until he tries them. Experiment is wide open, and the teacher must be pre-

Fig 10 Inspiration in the shapes of the materials.
Boy and girl, aged 13, make a bark and string construction

pared for any discovery the student makes. But (I can hear objections from countless teachers who have rescued themselves from more than one such chaotic situation!) it does not mean that the teacher has to stand by and watch a slow carnage taking over. Once the student has had time to consider the position and has shown what his intention is, the teacher can give any guidance he feels is needed, and can continue sharing in whatever progress the student makes. Certain aspects may have to be considered by the teacher and student together; but this can be done in such a way as to leave the student free to explore a range of solutions – not just one. Guidance should reshape an intention without upsetting it. It is better for a student to achieve at least some part of what he hoped for than that he should end up with an admirable piece of work he did not want.

The presented lesson

Let us take it that the teacher knows what he is aiming at in the lesson, and what he hopes to achieve through it. There is space for everyone to work, and enough materials and tools of the right kind ready to hand. He has decided how he will introduce the subject, e.g. by discussion or by something to look at or do, and what equipment he will need for this. He is clear about the ideas he wants to get across, and has a few leading questions to draw out as many students as he can (not just the few who always seem to answer). He should plan to cover the main points, but not go on too long or the initiative will be lost and interest flag: five minutes is usually long enough; it could be too long if the class can start earlier. He may keep the students fairly close to the idea in mind, or let it take other courses suggested by a turn of events or by the response of the students. Even a carefully prepared lesson can give way like this. Suppose, for example, that over a number of weeks the long-term plan is towards exploring the experience of 'being outdoors in different weathers': a sudden snowfall or thunderstorm or a rising fog, coinciding with the lesson, could give zest and point to it – even to going outside if it is possible. Or perhaps the plan is to investigate 'moving things': a fast wind comes up, driving smoke and leaves past the windows; a crane starts up on a nearby building site; jets roar over the roofs; or a moth is trapped, beating against the pane. The lesson could turn onto these incidents, using them as they are or as pointers to other ideas.

Whatever focus the lesson develops, the student should be able to adjust it and interpret what he finds. No two responses will be quite the same, for the experience will have a different meaning for everyone. One student may respond visually and be concerned with

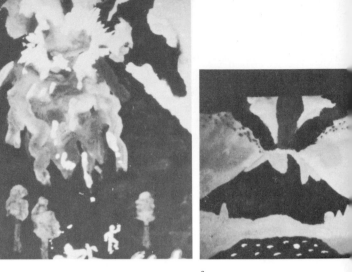

a b   c

Fig 11 Volcanos: girls aged 12

Fig 12 School building: boys aged 13

a

b c

32

the qualities he can see and touch. Another may become involved with a feeling that the experience arouses in him. Others may work from an idea or intuition it gives them. The illustrations in figs. 11, 12 show these different responses in representing a volcano, and in a study of the school building:

(a) mainly visual: the student has recorded the experience as being outside himself;

(b) emotional: he has interpreted it from a sense of being inside the experience, expressing it more as he feels it;

(c) as an idea: he has organized it according to a pattern already present in his mind.

Expression brings any number of sensibilities into play, but some may be more noticeable than others in the work of a particular student and help the teacher to understand what it means to him. If, for example, some of the class have become interested in the moth trapped in the window, a student responding visually may work solely from observation and represent the fluttering shape naturalistically. A student responding emotionally may identify more personally with the moth's predicament and express something of his own sensations through it. Other responses may lead to different interpretations, building up a number of superimposed images – perhaps from a knowledge of high-speed photography and carrying on into film making – or devising designs and constructions in various materials. Some students may discover nothing at all and be bored by the whole business. The teacher should allow 'escape routes' for them elsewhere.

The most contrived experience should be open to a variety of approaches. A rusty anchor is laid among sea debris – driftwood, cork, shells, seaweed, pebbles, a lobster pot, worn rope, trawl netting. Students may be drawn to it in various ways: by the shapes and the bleached, eroded surfaces; by the low harmonies of colour; by the feeling in it of sea things generally; by a broader memory of a half-forgotten event on a shore. The interest could well spread since texture and colour are not separate experiences, but belong to the same experience; and emotion is as visual as sight is emotional. The method of presentation should be such that it leaves the student to find his own way into the work, though the teacher may want to give it more direction by other means: recorded sea sounds, gulls, voices in the open; discussion around the origin and histories of the various objects and changes that have taken place in them. In fig. 13, the driftwood has suggested to the student the idea of a desolate landscape, and she has interpreted the forms imaginatively to help create the atmosphere.

If the objects had been bricks and pickaxes and builders' barrows

C

instead, or a neon sign blown down in a gale, similar thoughts could have followed. Imaginative subjects can also leave the door open to the various ways in which they can be seen, e.g. 'Out of control', 'Making animals', 'The earth is slipping', 'The last light in the city'.

The choice of media is part of the way of seeing. The anchor group may suggest drawing with a dry, crumbly medium like charcoal, painting with delicate washes, building up from torn paper as a collage, or as a construction in modelled and assembled materials. So with other subjects: the means of expression will come from the interest they awaken. Any range of materials will be realistic in terms of class numbers, space and time. Too wide a range can get out of hand; too narrow a range can exclude a student from the only interpretation that would have made sense for him. The student must be able to consolidate any strengths he has, but should be encouraged to try any new ones that could take his ideas further.

Fig 13 Driftwood landscape: girl aged 15

Simultaneous activities

If all the students are working with similar materials and processes the arrangements will be fairly straightforward. But if they are working with different ones, and possibly in different groups, the arrangements will call for further thought.

How does a teacher supervise several groups at the same time? The new teacher should be careful not to take on more than he can manage, giving himself time to get to know what is involved and, for a start, limiting the choice of media to two or three (say, one flat and one three-dimensional). With too many things going on, he would not be able to give each group the help they need at the right moment. Later on, he will feel he can let more happen and offer greater choice, but even this will depend on the space and arrangements in the room. He should probably try to group activities according to the main materials being used, so that wet and dry ones or those using specialist equipment, such as print-making, are kept apart as far as possible. If a noisy activity disturbs the rest, a quieter approach or a move can be considered.

The teacher should first of all see to those who will need least attention once they have started; then he can help the others begin, remaining with them until he is satisfied they can carry on alone. Throughout the lesson he should keep an eye on possible danger spots such as a heating glue kettle, cutting equipment, a wet-print rack, the sink. He may make individual students responsible for some of these, but he should not be lulled into thinking he can then forget them!

With several activities going on, the problem of controlling them becomes an interesting one. What does the teacher do about this? Keeping order is, first of all, a matter of personality – the teacher's mostly: the calm teacher will normally get a calm class, the well-organized teacher a well-organized class. Most students want him to be in control, though it may not always seem like it; and in general they respond to a situation they can see is planned for the smooth running of the class. This background planning is important – arrangements for separate working spaces, for apparatus and materials to be where they are wanted, for ease of movement, and so on. The class should understand such arrangements clearly: confusion about them can progress at an alarming speed from restlessness to total disorder. Any move in this direction should be halted at once and some kind of order re-established. Disorder is never far away from failing interest and the student who is bored quickly discovers how to undermine others who are getting on. The cause of the boredom could be with the lesson, the conditions, or the student himself; but if the student is interested in his work he will not be interested in upsetting others.

Fig 14 The materials are organized simply but effectively and the 'mess' is contained as the work develops

As for noise, the teacher should expect reasonable quietness while he is introducing or arranging a lesson, but once students are free to start, there will be things they need to say and do in getting ready. It is sensible to accept this noise at the beginning, though it should be kept below a level that would interfere with other classes or prevent the teacher making himself heard. He should recognize unnecessary noise and try to deal with the cause at once. Suppressing noise unduly at this stage could lead to it erupting in other forms later on during the lesson. Once groups have settled down to work, it is usually in everyone's interest to restore some degree of quiet. Silence is an uneasy state! Continuous noise does not as a rule make for good work, though it may be difficult to avoid at times, e.g. when all the class is using certain tools, or a project involves them in the exchange of ideas.

Finally, what about mess? Again, there is acceptable mess that comes with the ordinary use of materials – and there is unacceptable mess that comes from the misuse of them. This is a question of right methods, and one that can only be tackled on that level. Working mess, i.e. waste pieces, wet scrap paper, sawdust and so on, is part of the job and should be contained as the work goes along. Each student should keep an eye on the waste or mess from his work and clear it up from time to time. It soon accumulates and spreads, especially if it finds its way onto the floor.

Properly prepared and organized, wet media need not create much mess. There should be enough utensils of the right size and kind, and a quick way to the sink. Clay and plaster should not be walked across other parts of the room. Wet prints or paintings should be hung up at once out of the way. Oil media of any kind (printing or painting) should have their own separate facilities for clearing up. Resins, hot-water glue and other adhesives should be used so that they cannot get onto other work and spoil it.

Make sure that at least some of the following are available for clearing up: soft and hard brooms, a brush and dustpan, a fleece duster, large foam sponges, a scrubbing brush, a floor squeegee or mop, buckets, cloths – including separate ones for paraffin or white spirit – a scourer, broad palette knives, separate bins for wet and dry waste, heavy-duty polythene sheeting and plenty of old newspapers. Some processes (and students) take longer to clear up than others. This should begin in plenty of time for everyone to do his share and leave moments at the end for anything that has to be said about the lesson. The class, as a rule, should only leave when the room is clean and tidy and the work put away or left conveniently to dry.

4 The early years 11–14

Imagination and reality

In earlier chapters, I discussed the background of the new arrivals and what they feel lies before them in the art room. We already have a broad view of the adolescent when he arrives – at one extreme still expressive in his art; at the other, not expressive at all; and between the two, someone who is getting along with some degree of success. Apart from all that is going on in his private world – the clamourings and uncertainties of which we have spoken and which we can never fully know – there is, a little nearer the surface, a broader level of experience that we can see more clearly. Wherever he stands, the adolescent is now sharing with his friends a new outlook which is expressed in his attitude to imagined and real experience. Not so very long ago, he might have found it difficult to draw with confidence the line between what he imagined and what was more apparent from evidence round about him. The experiences were incautiously and, for the most part, convincingly mixed. But it was becoming clear that they were indeed two different kinds of experience, and that in some way the imagined ones that he could believe in or reject as he chose were separating from those he could not, and which he had to accept as they were. They had not come so far that either had taken over completely, but he was falling more into the way of one kind of thinking than the other, and this was reflected in much of the expressive work he was doing.

For one student, the heroic and bewitched country of earlier childhood may still be strongly influencing his conceptions. He may have detached himself from its themes and characters, but he projects them into his present world in different forms with an imagery that is just as personal and highly coloured, though with more attention possibly to detail. The giants and magic happenings of yesterday are finding a new stature and mystery in the images he makes from his new experience: an unconquered mountain, a skyscraper, a traveller in space, or a haunted tenement may take over the part and assume all the significance of his previous statements. For another youngster, however, the things he sees around him may have overtaken his earlier conceptions. He is attracted more to record and interpret what he finds, and will be likely to develop towards greater naturalism in his work.

It often happens that an adolescent becomes shy about his imaginative work and turns to kinds that are less revealing. He may, nevertheless, still be really more at home with his imagination than with the facts and appearances of things as they are. These are not two distinct paths: imagination enters into the simplest recorded work, as seeing and feeling do into imaginative work. But a certain weight can be sensed on one side or the other from the way experiences are interpreted. The particular vision that a boy or girl has at this age is the mainspring of any real creative growth that will take place from now on. It follows that there should be room for either kind of work, and that a different encouragement is called for if each is to develop. This does not mean that there should be one incentive for imaginative work and another for objective (though this could happen) – but that any class experience should be open to either: one may help the other. However, it is far from true that a searching study of the environment necessarily helps the imagination. The very opposite is often true: it can inhibit it. Art can be deeply personal and not connected in any way with the study of outward things. Such a study could direct the imaginative conception to the likeness and relationship of forms as they are seen, and 'correct' any attempt to represent them differently. A falling-off on one side is only significant if it is felt to limit expression generally. The teacher can offer any incentive he feels is right to help the student over such a difficulty.

To which areas of the imagination does the adolescent return again and again? Some are private ones where he is alone with his heroes and his dreams and his questions about himself. Others are public ones where he adventures outside: games, secret ceremonies, gang territory, animals, birds. These are things he knows about: he may create instinctively, and can be left to it with just the materials and tools he needs; he may, more often, want someone to suggest a way into them. This is where the teacher comes in, opening up an idea which the student can recognize.

What are these ideas that the teacher can fairly confidently suggest?

1 Heroes, legends, mysteries, in which the central characters or events are larger than life. In fig. 15, the knight is doing battle with superior forces in an assault on a castle – and is clearly winning.
2 Dreams – mixing fact and fantasy, and where anything can happen. Fig. 16 shows a dream in which the sleeper walks across the spires of a city.
3 The student's picture of himself, the people and everyday events around him; adventures he has alone or with others. Fig. 17 is a self-portrait, painted with observation and humour; fig. 18 is of a favourite haunt, a used-car dump where games and secret meetings regularly take place; fig. 19 is a newspaper collage making use of banner headlines and print areas to build up the picture of a pop group.
4 Great occasions: parades, carnivals, ceremonies, rituals, give chances for decorative staging, ornate costume and accessories.

Fig. 15 Boy aged 13

Fig. 16 Boy aged 13

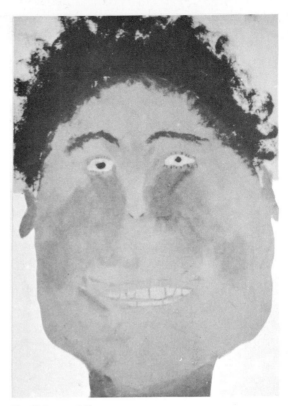

Fig. 17 Boy aged 11

Fig. 18 Boy aged 12

Fig. 19 Girls aged 11

5 Wild landscape – its moods and drama. See cover illustration.
6 Animals, birds and other creatures, real or imaginary. In fig. 20 the student is finishing a lizard suggested by the twisting shapes of a hedgerow root; fig. 27 shows a many-headed sea-monster threatening the sailors in their boat.

How the teacher leads into any of these ideas makes a difference to the way the class interprets it. What he says or brings out in discussion should draw the students in as they each begin to see it in their own way.

There is a chance that by over-stressing one aspect or approach, the teacher could carry students too far away from a direction they might have found more expressive. If, for example, the idea was about a great hero (and everyone has his own) the introduction should deal in wider terms with personal bravery, presence, bearing and so on, and not linger on any particular hero or kind of heroism – unless it was one the whole class was interested in. The teacher

Fig. 20 Boy aged 13

might also use certain aids or go through actions associated with the idea. 'A great occasion' might suggest inventing and staging an event on the spot ('A tournament', 'The opening of the first space station', 'Visit of the Black Queen', 'The wedding of the gypsies': fig. 22 shows some of the class dressed up and acting out such an occasion). If the idea is to develop from a deeper imaginative level, such a presentation would be too forceful, though some students may still be helped by seeing and handling materials and other accessories left around for draping or putting on.

Again, to over-stress any visual aspect could lead to its indiscriminate use, and either way might focus attention on it out of keeping with the spirit of the work as a whole. Furthermore, it does not play a big part in the response of students whose work develops more from other sources, and it would be better to underplay such incentives than to make too much of them. This is true for any stimulus. A subject such as 'Adventure in the Antarctic' would gain little in realism and lose much in feeling from too pointed a study

43

Fig. 21 'Defence of a narrow bridge'

Fig 22 'Wedding of the gypsies'

of snow that has been falling in the grounds – though this may indeed have inspired the subject initially. The fact that the snow is there at all is probably enough. Under other circumstances, as in dealing with 'being outdoors' (page 31), more use could be made of it.

With these thoughts in mind, however, acting-out an episode will usually make for a lively start. A student can identify with the movements and gestures by going through them or watching them, and can carry the feeling into his work. 'Defending a narrow bridge single-handed' can be done with a ruler between two close rows of chairs and with half-a-dozen classmates advancing through them (fig. 21). Or 'Folding a big sheet' can be managed by two girls using nothing but their imagination. 'Folding a tent in a high wind' would tease the inventiveness of the actors and the audience even more. The rest of the picture can always be completed freely, and even go far beyond the original intention.

In trying to imagine a picture from a conventional viewpoint, a student is often faced with the same problems that have cropped up before with similar subjects: the old stylizations *will* keep reappearing and getting in the way of the picture he wants to make. But if he tries to represent it from an unusual point of view, he has to approach it in a way that almost unthinkingly breaks up the old restrictive forms, e.g. a city area as a pigeon sees it; what harvesting looks like to a field vole; fishing through the fishes' eyes or a flower through a bee's.

Other incentives may also be important. Sound, for example, plays a big part in responses and imagination: actual sounds like chanting a familiar game to conjure up a picture of it; recorded sounds, like a vixen's cry at night to call up the image of a dark countryside, or pin-tables that of an amusement arcade; military music to create the mood of marching – all may have their use, particularly for the student with a strong sense of sound associations. In the same way, touch, smell and taste experiences have their place. The adolescent's emotional life is becoming more complicated and involving him in complex responses. Sense impressions have increasing emotional significance or undertones, and can stir deep personal feelings.

A student who has given up his own attempts and fallen back on copying ideas may end up depicting subjects in the manner of illustrations he has seen. This suggests that his own interest is not strong enough for him to say anything original: in which case, the attempt will have little meaning for him. But it may be that he only needs to discover his own attitude to a subject, and a word or two from the teacher may give him the right start. In fig. 23, the cartoon

Fig. 23 Boys aged 13/14

idiom has found a more personal expression in clay modelling.

There is little doubt that most adolescents want at some time or other to be able to draw convincingly, both as they see and as they imagine things. It is hardly enough just to acknowledge this: the need should be met in the actual planning of the lessons.

Objects

The adolescent is already noticing more about the shapes and colours around him. His everyday world is one of forms that he sees and touches and handles. There are places where they are found, and places where it would be strange to find them. What they are like in one environment is not quite what they are like in another, for they always take something of their character from it and contribute to it in return. A can of beans in a food cupboard is not the same as a can of beans outdoors: the effect is different. Fishing gear in a store is not the same as it is at home or by a river. A chair removed from under a table and put among other chairs breaks one association (with the table) and sets up another (with the chairs): one's feeling about it alters, just as its physical appearance does. At

Fig. 24 Boy aged 12. Fruit treated imaginatively

the same time, the table and the other chairs also seem different.

Any study of forms should surely start here, in the setting around them; and the teacher should encourage the student to look for understanding in this way. It is doubtful whether there is much value in detaching a single object and making a study of it in isolation, though it could be argued that it has qualities of its own and can be explored by itself, developing a particular presence in that way. Only interest and curiosity, however, should draw a student into his search among the world of objects. If these are missing, the search has no point; and, from a purely perfunctory study, he can at best go through the unwilling motions. The trouble is that much of art education and examination syllabuses give such weight and sanction to 'object studies'. For the wrong student, whose gifts lie in other directions, this kind of study could be an actual risk and hold him back from his more natural forms of expression (fig. 24). For the student who is interested and curious, the search can be surprising and eventful. But where does it lie? And how can the teacher help?

Excursions into other parts of the school and grounds may open up all kinds of discovery; but these are not always possible. It may depend largely on the teacher having a variety of objects circulating in the room. This does not mean that it should be littered with bric-a-brac and the sad remnants of nature left to gather dust and become part of the furniture – but that there should be times when unexpected things 'appear' and invite investigation. In fig. 25, the teacher has taken the opportunity to introduce a lobster pot. The cavity forms created by the cordage echo the feeling of some hollowed terracotta heads that have been made, and he has set them

Fig. 25 Boy and girl aged 13

all up together. It is an arresting comparison, and a new object has found its way into the room. Complex and unusual shapes are often a greater incentive than simple ones, though both have their place and can offer new experiences by the way in which they are presented. Objects that have turned up in various art rooms include such things as parts of old farm machinery, rocks and driftwood, an iron coal-face wheel, ship's gear and tackle, a wicker bull's head, an electrical circuit panel, a giant cactus, heavy coloured glass chunks, a Victorian smoothing iron, a Sanscrit prayer-board, a cathode tube, old lace, a station clock-face, blacksmith's bellows, an early doll, lock mechanism from an old church door and a bank vault – and more than once, an object no one could identify. But such things must never be allowed to overstay their welcome: they should be pointers to other things that lie outside.

The teacher and the students between them will be able to collect a lot of pieces that bring the outside world into the art room for a while. The most familiar object can take on startling dimensions and qualities just by being seen in a different context or by unusual

Fig. 26 The school pet

lighting (a lamp with a wandering lead is useful for this, since windows and installed lights are not always conveniently placed). The teacher can help the student feel for the 'personality' of an object – something of its special character and its private world – which he can then try to express rather than just making a literal copy. Touching and feeling an object belong to the experience. Sometimes quite a small thing 'owned' by the student for a while, can help him associate with it and express it better. In many cases, his interest will carry him beyond any one view. The answer here may lie in modelling or carving, or in a series of drawings made from various positions or with a number of different media. Any unusual surface provides a fresh starting-point (painting on grained wood is different from painting on cardboard). This all applies equally in the case of plants and animals and people. But again, the teacher has to manage largely in the world of the art room, and will have to do what he can there. In fig. 26, a school pet has been brought in. It expects attention and makes itself at home among the students.

Fig. 27 Girls aged 11/12

Fig 28 Hiding the figure

The figure

Many of the student's enquiries centre more around people, and the figure becomes a challenge or a threat that he cannot avoid.

The prospect of a figure just sitting or standing seldom arouses much excitement at this stage. At best, the student will probably only manage an inert reproduction of the pose. It is often too close in appearance to the schematic figure of his earlier years, which no longer satisfies him, and it leads him back into the older form that worries him now because it looks unreal. Unless he can break with this, he will be unable to develop the human figure expressively in his work as a whole, and may omit it altogether. This shuts him off from one of the great adventures he could have had, especially as so many of his conceptions are coming to include the figure as he sees it. Something more is needed to stir his curiosity and understanding.

This 'something' may be no more than a dress change: period dress from the school drama wardrobe if there is one, or from a drama organization in the area which might be willing to lend it; tradesmen's clothes or uniforms, e.g. air hostess, commissionaire, nurse, patrol man, borrowed perhaps from friends or the students' families; fancy or party dress; national or dance costumes; or even

50

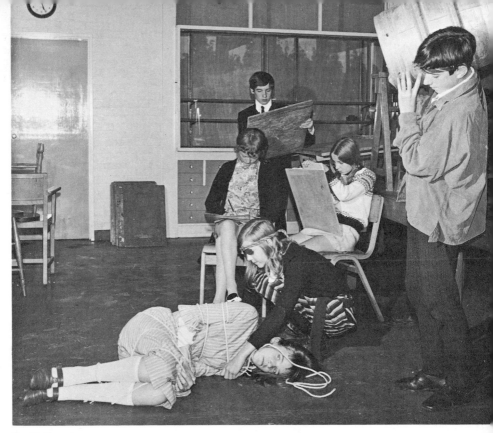

Fig. 29 The prisoner

just odd drapes such as coloured blankets, towels, shawls, travelling rugs. Even simple changes in ordinary wear are often enough in themselves, e.g. a coat worn back-to-front. Studies of this kind can turn into pictures or sculpture of any event the clothes suggest.

The teacher can arrange for the model to dress out of sight of the class and make a surprise entrance, with the advantage of impact; or to do so openly, allowing time perhaps for a quick sketch at each stage. An arrested action catches the attention and prompts lively work. Students could exchange their impressions and pass round the papers as each drawing is finished, building up a number of composite pictures.

Another way is to cover the model completely with a large sheet, out of sight of the class (fig. 28). In itself, this is an interesting study; but to attempt the figure further as it is imagined *under* the sheet opens up all kinds of speculation and experiment. A partly-concealed figure is also open to conjecture. A figure trussed up with cord, apart from its entertainment value, invites an exploration of the forms in the way the cords wind – and perhaps in a wider context, e.g. 'Caught by smugglers' (fig. 29). A situation where a

51

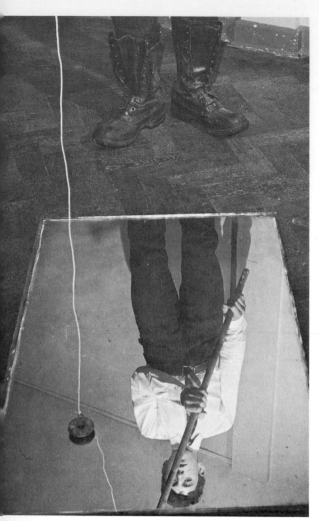

Fig 30 The 'pool'
Fig. 31 A few accessories suggest the incident

figure is doing something brings it to life, e.g. mending a tyre puncture, being a fireman, getting impatient, falling off a chair (accessories can also help, e.g. a bicycle, a tangled hosepipe – fig. 31).

Using a sheet and a back light, one or two students could act out a shadow mime like 'Boxing' or 'Putting on make-up'. The rest of the class see the figure shapes without being worried too much by detail, and can, as before, develop the action imaginatively. Paper collage could interpret the shapes more directly *as* shapes. If a student is held back by an earlier, fixed way of drawing, it is often seen in the way he handles proportions and articulation; the teacher can help by getting him to act out movements for himself, feeling and seeing what is happening as he does so. Many indoor and outdoor experiments can be devised, using other equipment such as large mirrors or mirror glass, which can easily be 'a pool'

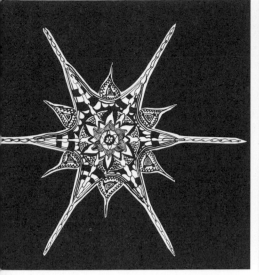

Fig. 32 Designs that grow with different pens and brushes. Girls aged 11/12

reflecting someone standing over it, or serve more conventional purposes (fig. 30).

A student should be able to develop any life study in the direction it takes him. The search is what he finds, not necessarily what he set out to find. Stress on any form of inertia-copying can easily upset the student who may have his own fantasy or lyrical interpretation of the figure.

The stimulus of new media

Last but not least, there is the stimulus of the materials themselves. Earlier and often persisting habits of bold work with media contrast now with more restrained approaches, from reasons either of true feeling or of caution. In picture-making, both approaches will be met by a range of broad and fine media: charcoal, conté, wax crayon, pen and ink, chalks, felt (and U.K., fibre) tip pens, poster colour, tempera paste, and water-colour; an assortment of brushes, painting and palette knives, and paint spreaders improvised from pieces of plastic, wood or thin metal, all producing different effects. In the same way, different surfaces can be a new experience: papers of unusual size, colour or texture, cardboard (new and scrap), hardboard, insulation board, wood panels, roofing materials, asbestos and stretched fabrics. Some of the hard surfaces are more inviting when they are primed with an emulsion paint or gesso, or when a textured fabric is glued to them. Sand, slate dust and similar materials can also be used to texture them.

The introduction of new processes is now becoming urgent as an incentive to drawing. Where accustomed ones have come to produce the same disappointing results, an untried process will often give the work new qualities. Such processes include wax

Fig. 33 Boy aged 12

Fig. 34 Boy aged 11

Fig. 35 Girl aged 13

etching, i.e. engraving through layers of wax crayoning to the surface beneath, or through paint applied over the crayoning (powder colour in a little neat detergent covers well); drawing with a candle or melted wax onto a surface and washing colour over it; engraved drawing on a colour-washed plaster slab or on other surfaces like flat slate; drawing with a brush dipped in a fluid adhesive, with powder or sand sprinkled over it and the excess shaken off to leave the drawing in low relief; drawing with a blunt point onto an inked plate and taking a monoprint from it (fig. 33); drawing through paper onto an inked plate so that the work comes out on the underside (fig. 34); drawing with thread or wire (fig. 35: interest in a medieval manuscript illustration led to a new experience with thread). Many other experimental uses of media can be discovered. In fig. 37, for example, paper has been laid on a potter's banding wheel, and a brush of paint held to it. The designs grow as the wheel turns.

But interest is turning more towards other kinds of materials. This is an age of developing three-dimensional experiments when the adolescent is coming to grips with his physical environment largely through handling and shaping. Three-dimensional materials are part of it. He can get at them directly – physically. He can feel for the shapes in them and for how they might assemble. And there are tools to use: what they do to the materials gives him ideas as he goes along. He can manage them better now, and judge whether they are suitable for a certain job. He can accept the discipline the material imposes, where he would resent other kinds of discipline

Fig 36   Fig 37

Fig. 36 Strips of card hooked together as a relief. Effects change under moving coloured lights.
      Boy aged 12
Fig. 37 Girl aged 13

that imply criticism. A new process can bring out abilities that never showed as long as he was only using a crayon or a brush.

Suitable materials include: various kinds of flat scrap and natural materials: fabric pieces, corrugated card, builders' left-overs and off-cuts, metal foils, dry leaves, seeds and plants, bark etc. for making collages; also wood, metal, glass, containers, machine parts, pebbles, shells etc., for making mounted reliefs, mosaics and constructions (fig. 36, 38). Sources are inexhaustible: the home, basements and attics, the workshop, the local tip or junk yard, nearby factories, country lanes and the sea-shore. The materials themselves will often suggest a subject and, used in various ways together, can release all kinds of inventive thinking. *They are not a substitute for traditional materials but invite a different quality of seeing and making; there is as much creative integrity in their use as in any medium.*

Materials for modelling or pottery: home-dug and prepared clays, plastic modelling materials, plaster (with scrim) for modelling onto an armature, experimental modelling mixtures such as pulped papier mâché with plaster.

Materials for carving: soft brick, builders' cement block, chalk lumps, hard dried clay, driftwood, branches, logs, sandstone, lime-stone, plaster block cast in a disposable container, expanded poly-styrene (U.S. styrofoam), paraffin wax, soap, cuttlefish bone, soft woods such as balsa, North American yellow pine, lime, cedar, birch.

Materials for printmaking: objects, blocks or simple screens from which to print, and a variety of printing papers and fabrics. The appeal of this craft lies partly in the processes and partly in the unexpected effects. Different coloured printing papers, including tissues, can be as surprising as different coloured inks, and not as expensive (fig. 39).

Materials for other crafts like puppetry, embroidery, tie-dyeing, wax resist, mobiles, photography and film making.

Tools for shaping or fixing the materials will be needed, including a range of adhesives (see my book *Creative Crafts for Today*,

56

Fig. 38 Low relief of broken china. Girl aged 14

Fig. 39 Monoprint. Boy aged 14

Studio Vista). The implications of using untried materials are dicussed on page 26.

Among the chief reasons for introducing these materials is that they offer an immediate means of expression, i.e., the student can translate a three-dimensional experience, say of a figure or an animal, straight into a three-dimensional medium, making it at once easier to imagine. A portrait of Captain Scott or Buffalo Bill or the Three Wise Men is likely to be more exciting and successful worked out as a fabric collage or a model in plaster than it would be as a drawing. 'An imaginary creature' can take shape better from scrap pieces and driftwood than from a brush. 'Birth' and 'Death' can be carved with new feeling from wood or a building block. Modelling a figure in clay encourages a livelier sense of its forms and movement, and allows for changes in it as it grows. The clay is flexible, as the body is, and can be bent or pulled, squeezed or filled out to express shape and action – though always within the working properties of the clay (this is the discipline found in the material, and one that would be different if cane or wire or plastic were used instead). Making a string puppet can also help with problems of movement and articulation.

Group work
Because young people of this age tend naturally to form into small groups on their own, and to move towards more involvement with others, there is a real place during these years for the group project. Whether this means working together on a mural (fig. 40), or contributing individual pieces to a group theme (fig. 42), there are many ways in which it can help: the student can work more confidently as one of a team, especially if he is worried about what he achieves on his own; his work can merge with that of others, and gain from being part of an overall affect; he will learn from others without necessarily copying them – the social nature of the occasion keeps ideas circulating informally; and finally, the group project can achieve a greater scale than any student could manage alone. The teacher should try to bring students in at whatever level they can contribute, though new aptitudes could come to light in the course of the work. These are useful guides for the future. No student should be compelled to take part, but if the teacher feels it would help him, he will undoubtedly find ways of encouraging him to do so.

1 *A mural* worked straight onto a wall as a painting or collage, or on a board or paper for mounting later. A theme is agreed, and all the students tackle what parts they can.

2 *'Series' pictures:* a sequence of episodes in a planned story, with one or more students doing each picture. This again can be done directly on a wall or mounted afterwards as a frieze.

3 *A class book* with planned contributions (illustrations, script, binding).

4 *Printmaking:* individuals make their own prints for assembling into a larger design, e.g. views into the windows of apartment buildings: each 'window print' is mounted with others to form the façade.

5 *A panorama or tableau:* e.g. a landscape made from scrap or modelling and carving materials (fig. 41); or a zoo, with each student making his own animal and helping generally with cages, etc. The business of relating the various parts to each other keeps the work at discussion level.

6 *A large construction* (fine for outdoors!) using scrap or traditional materials, fired clay work, etc. Ideas and assembly skills are shared at all stages.

Fig. 40 Group wall painting for a social studies room, Boys aged 11/12

Fig 41 Modelling mountains from paper, fabric and plaster — a corner of a larger landscape project to which the class contribute whatever features interest them. Later on, creatures made from leaves, shavings, metal and other scrap can become part of a prehistoric drama in the valleys and river beds. Boys, girls aged 11

7 *Puppetry:* apart from making and contributing individual puppets to a production, there are other sides to this that make it a good group activity (building and equipping the theatre, writing a script, devising sound effects, performing).

8 *Film-making:* there is similar scope for different kinds of contribution.

Fig. 42 Fired clay modelling. Six students each make a musician for an orchestra. Boys, girls aged 12

Outside pursuits

The adolescent can sometimes be drawn into expressive work through his own personal interests outside school – stamp collecting, Scouting, camping, dressmaking, sport, model aircraft, tropical fish, electronics and so on. In fig. 43, the student has painted a mural in the school corridor arising from his interest in model aircraft. Pictures on stamps may suggest a theme that could be expanded imaginatively. Scouting may involve a boy in animal tracking that, in turn, could give rise to an animal or countryside subject. Dressmaking could lead to other inventive uses of fabrics and machining. The possibilities are endless once the search is begun,

Fig. 43 Boy aged 15

and projects that connect with an enthusiasm of this kind will have greater validity for the student.

This gives rise to thoughts about the contacts between the home and the school. The parents know the family interests: the teacher knows what the son or daughter could attempt at school. Between them, they may discover many ways of enlarging on what he is busy with at the moment.

The student should at the same time be looking at any art and constructive work that gives him a feeling for life through other eyes and for the rich variety of things men make. Such things as:

1 The popular and decorative arts of the town and countryside – shop fronts, sign boards, public lettering, amusement arcades, film sets, theatres, fairgrounds, caravans and barges, parade banners and costumes, civic arms, etc.
2 Buildings and building sites, bridges, public works and services, industrial complexes.
3 Works in public and private collections, studio workshops and factories.
4 Illustrated books.

In this way the young student is coming to terms with the world of his imagination, and the world as it is around him. With encouragement and experiment, he can continue to find satisfaction in expressing both.

High and low ability
From time to time, every teacher has in his classes the student with outstanding creative ability and the one with apparently no ability at all.

The gifted student may appear to need little help beyond a word or two about what he intends to do and any process that will be involved. He can then carry on by himself, quickly finding his own expressive use of the materials. It is always a pleasure to have a student doing brilliant work, but the teacher should guard against leaving him alone too much or spending too much time with him. He should let him get on as far as he can, but be prepared to discuss the progress of the work at any point if it becomes necessary.

The student may excel in many other subjects as well as art, and be equally interested in all of them. Or he may become more interested in art and decide to specialize. The teacher can usefully guide him in this and give the right assistance whichever course he takes up. In the case of another student, however, art may be his one strong point; and, as much of his confidence rests with this, he should be able to develop his skills here to the full. They could well help him in the end with his other subjects (see chapter on 'Sources in other subjects').

The student may have creative flair for any medium he uses and will broaden his field with each attempt, though the teacher will watch that he really is extending, not being led into mere technical exuberance. A student who shows exceptional ability only in certain media could nevertheless be discovering a remarkable depth of vision through them, and can be left to the adventures they offer him. The teacher will notice occasions when progress depends on attempting a new medium.

The teacher can encourage a talent better if he knows something of the student's background. Has he been helped to develop it over the years? What kind of help has he had? Has he met with opposition or indifference? What effect have these had on his work? The value of the teacher's attitude may hinge on his understanding of this. Useful incentives for the gifted student include:

Large-scale work, destined perhaps for a selected place in the school.

Development of a theme through a series of different media.

Use of more specialized processes.

Design and supervision of stage or film sets, or of decor in connection with some other school activity.

Arrangements for a special exhibition of the student's work in or outside the school.

The student may be planning to go on to further education or into an art career when he leaves school. Even with this in mind, he should continue developing along his own lines and not try to anticipate any work he will be taking up eventually.

The student with practically no creative ability at all also needs special help. He may have low all-round ability in other subjects, or just be particularly weak in art. In either case, the teacher can help him by making the most of any small success he can manage. This could be very small indeed at times, and hardly count for much by any other standard; but it will give him enough confidence to try something else later. He may only be able to tackle a particular kind of subject or medium. If so, he should keep to these until they suggest a way through into some other kind. It is far better to build in these areas than make renewed and fruitless departures from them. He could fail again and again, for example, to produce a satisfactory painting or model, but he might just be able to make an attractive pattern which could lead later into a simple mosaic using pottery fragments, small pebbles or chips of coloured formica.

These in turn could draw him into further experiments with the materials on different lines.

In many instances, low creative ability is the result of difficulties encountered in the past, and a new experience may be all that is needed to bring out a hidden talent. Progress will almost certainly be slow however, and the teacher will have to follow up every advantage he discovers to put the student at ease and set him on the track of some rewarding kind of work.

5 The later years 14–18

No line divides the lower school from the upper: there is no frontier the adolescent crosses – the steps are gradual and different for everyone. A class moves up the school with some students ahead and some falling back in the various things they do, including art. As before, there are those who continue to meet the changes taking place; and others who, still dealing with earlier problems, are faced with yet further ones as they are caught up too fast in the adult world. For a student like this, new dilemmas are lining up. What absorbed him once is not absorbing any more; ideas he held until quite recently are going overboard; he sees what he is doing in the light of new, dimly-forming attitudes.

The outward search and the inner questioning
Imagination and reality may now be falling clearly into more conventional camps, with imagination on one side, being more or less capricious and speculative – not to be taken too seriously – and reality on the other, made up of the physical and emotional facts on which everyone agrees.

In some ways, imaginative work has now come under even graver suspicion, with its departure from the conventions of seeing and feeling. It rings uneasy bells, reminding him of younger days, casting doubt on his representational abilities. Now he is more knowledgeable about himself and his relationships with others, and at the same time less sure of himself and affected more by criticism. As a result he often feels safer working in areas not so open to it – areas, that is, of straightforward representation. By turning his attention away from himself and on to the outside world, he is not under the same pressure to bring his private thoughts and fantasies into play.

For this and other quite natural reasons, representation is becoming one of the main driving forces. He concentrates more on achieving life-like effects as he sees them and knows them to be recognizable. For one adolescent, this stress on visual accuracy only underlines the nature of his true response, and he may in fact always have worked like this. For *any* student, however, it is at least an unmistakeable attainment. The result can be 'tested' against the fact and shown to be right or wrong, unlike results of a more personal kind which cannot. But the teacher may have to save such a student from becoming caught up in a chase after visual prizes when his real path lies elsewhere. Perhaps the student himself knows that what he wants to say has nothing to do with how things appear, and that arduous recording takes him further and further away from saying it. But alone, he may not escape being carried along by the main drift: he would have to be very confident

Fig. 44 Day draws into night. Girl aged 17

in his own way of expression to resist it. The teacher has to help him value his vision, whatever it is, and sustain him in it – not easy for either of them, but the only way if the work is to continue to mean anything.

For this reason, the teacher must promote work on all fronts, openly encouraging the student to create emotionally from what emotion creates in him. Figs. 44, 45 express different students' feelings about the turning point when day moves into night, and natural light is confused with more glaring artificial ones. Fig. 49 is the feeling of being frightened. Fig. 50 is 'getting a shock from an electric light socket'. The teacher must draw the student into a deepening enquiry into the forces and circumstances that affect him, following up ideas with experiment and experiment with ideas – taking a thought as far as it needs through any sequence of tests with materials. The thought may come unexpectedly from the past; it may have been present for some time; it may come from what is happening at the moment. The process is untraceable: but it might be the right moment now to express it . . .

Fig. 45 Day draws into night. Girl aged 18

Fig. 46 Boys aged 15/16

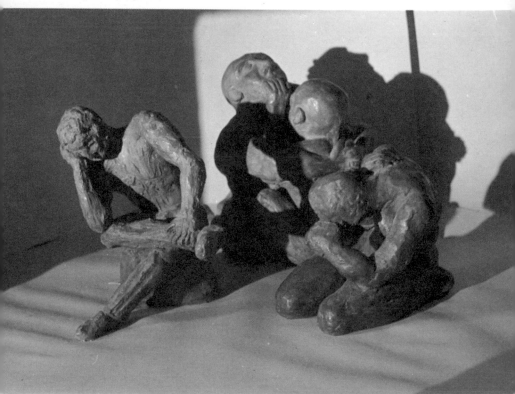

Fig. 47 Boy aged 14

Fig. 48 A 7 ft high sculpture. It began life as a little maquette in offcuts. The student thought it would be good to be able to walk around in it and carried out this larger version in square section steel tube and hardboard, fixed with split pins. The wind finally blew it down after the school had enjoyed its spacial experience. Boy aged 17

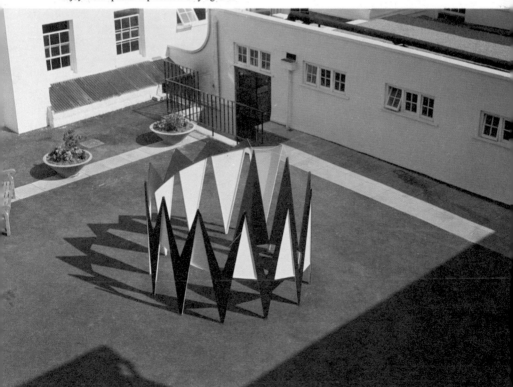

Fig. 49 Being frightened. Boy aged 14   Fig. 50 Getting an electric shock. Boy aged 14

There is fruit tumbled on an art room table; sunlight falls on the table, and all the colours glow in it . . . oranges, lemons, pine-apple, cherries, melon. It is there for painting – for those who will make for their paints when they see it. But what of the student who is unaffected in that way? Seeing the fruit may trigger an association of ideas and memory deeper than ideas of glowing colour and the shapes before him '. . . orange . . . lemon . . . cherries . . . FRUIT MACHINE . . . the coin drops . . . spinning pictures . . . catch them at the right one – three oranges in a row (*that* would be tidy, and a gush and clatter coming out the bottom) . . . if only it would! . . . but it won't! . . . dead clonk . . . NOTHING . . . BANG IT and hate it . . . love it . . . do it again – make all that machinery start working for me again . . . listen for the cascade – lovely noise . . . all that counting . . . love to pull the handle, rock the lever . . . kickstart's broken on my bike – left it at Jim's last night . . . have to walk home . . .'

Somewhere along the line the sight, the sensation, the sense of occasion, the feel and the touch, the certainty and the risk all bear on the experience. Anywhere along the line expression could take over and give shape to a moment in it. What form will it take – colour, metal cans and rubber rollers, soft clay, hard plastic, bits of machinery and living fruit? Are there things around that he can use or get? Will it be all right with the teacher? He might be able to do it – this time, next time. If there is no 'this time', there may not be a next time . . .

70

The fruit is still on the table. There are a few students painting it. Another is not. He is remembering other oranges he has
had . . . peeling them (an odd feeling, like peeling off a wet swim-
suit – white underneath, like skin that's missed the suntan) . . .
break open the sections of the orange (why are they like that, all
symmetrical, all round an axis in the same way, pulled up close
to each other, yet separate?) . . . an orbital tension . . . make up
segments out of something (balsa, moulded cardboard, plastic),
link them with elastic so they snap shut in a tight globe . . . (anything
to do with seed arrangement, fair shares of nourishment, a survival
shape) . . . smell from the orange peel as sharp as ammonia – bitter,
a bit sweet – like suntan lotion when you get a taste by accident . . .

Where do his thoughts carry him? The questions may stop anywhere and experiments start. The teacher cannot know. He can
only make room for the thoughts and time for the experiments. Or
he may go further. He may be able to stir responses of these kinds,
especially if he feels they lie just below the surface anyway. He may
be able to draw the emotions and the reasoning from under cover.
If the experiments are just passing ones, leaving no evidence, they
will at least have happened: that is important. They could be experiments with water and air and heat, setting materials and ideas
in motion – coloured liquids, balloons, kites, wind and water vanes,
light and sound effects. Expression may need this help: it may only
come about when activity starts. All kinds of forces are at work in
the class: they cannot be ignored. The teacher can go quite a way
towards releasing them.

But there still remains the strong urge to record what the eye
sees. In the main, this is increasing for the older adolescent. He is
finding himself more and more an observer of a rapidly enlarging
world outside himself. It is all coming to exist as something apart,
and he is led to represent it at its face value – which means in terms
of the shape, colour, perspective and other relationships of things.

Although the student is dealing with something outside himself,
each attempt to represent it brings it more inside his experience,
and enables him to define and grasp at least a little of the changing
scene around him. Each attempt may be picked up elsewhere in
some future experience and will heighten his sense of that experience;
for example, from painting objects in a window light, he will see
objects in other windows with something of the presence that these
developed for him in the course of his painting; and the way he
manages to describe their forms and colours will carry an awareness of these qualities into similar occasions.

It can not be expected that in the art lessons alone, probably
shorter or less frequent now, a student can explore in more than a

E

few directions or that he can do so at much depth. He may be quite happy to carry on from lesson to lesson at his own speed with his own ideas, but other students may need guiding towards experiences they can manage in the time available. With this in mind, the teacher might map out a few broad areas to explore:

The human situation – the figure.

The outdoor and indoor worlds – their freedoms and limits, their structure and features.

Animal and plant worlds.

Given a start, more of the students will be able to make their own way through observation or feeling and need little more than to be noticed occasionally. One piece of work may lead naturally into another as thoughts connect and ideas grow. In deciding on a theme, the teacher should try to keep as close as possible to the students' own life – figures doing something (fig. 46), places the students have explored, that have character or atmosphere (figs. 47, 51–53), animals they know (fig. 54), objects they use. By doing so, he will be more likely to encourage personal thinking about it – and from

Fig. 51 A local factory. Collage using candy separators and pressed leaves. Boy aged 16

Fig. 52 Girl aged 15

this, personal interpretation. In the long run, this is the kind of guidance that will see the student through; but from time to time, he may need practical and immediate help in focusing on an experience, e.g. deciding what it is that gives a particular figure or form its effect (its movement, weight, balance, surfaces, colour, construction, lighting and so on).

Naturally, an environment study of this sort grows out of earlier work, and any of the earlier incentives may still be useful. Further incentives, however, will be needed for the older student. With his fuller sense of relationships, the *grouping* of figures and objects is now coming to be important. Figures acting as models could form into a group all at once, or come in a few at a time to make up a larger group, the first ones remaining or retiring according to how

Fig. 53 Girl aged 17

Fig. 54 Girl aged 17

Fig. 55 Boy aged 14

Fig. 56 Girl aged 16

the event is managed. In fig. 55, the models have posed as a group, and the quick resulting sketch is finished imaginatively as the scene of a street accident. In figs. 56, 57 the models pose one at a time and are drawn in more detail. Interest lies not only in the different groupings but in the varieties of build, dress and posture. Themes might develop like 'The Local Dancehall', with some students as dancers and others as onlookers, sitting or standing around (fig. 59). 'A Basketball or Baseball Incident' might introduce figures into a given action-situation – the more strenuous the pose, the quicker the study.

Other incentives: unusual lighting, e.g. from below, or using coloured light; the use of tall mirrors to reflect and re-reflect views; staging physical states like balance, fatigue, strain, exercise – with the help of any apparatus needed (fig. 58). There should still be chances for the student to make more studied drawings and paintings of the figure (figs. 61, 62).

Fig. 57 Girl aged 16

Fig. 58 Lifting each other. All kinds of experience can be acted out by the students

Fig. 59 'At the local dance'

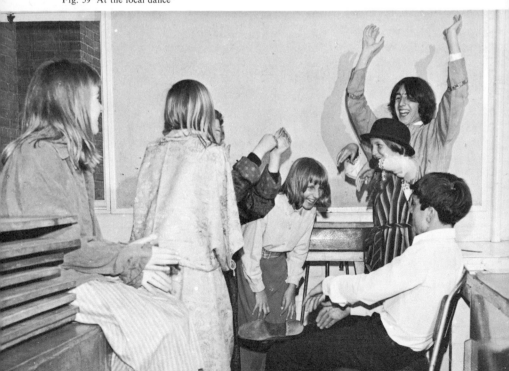

Fig. 60 A painting can develop from action poses. Girl aged 16

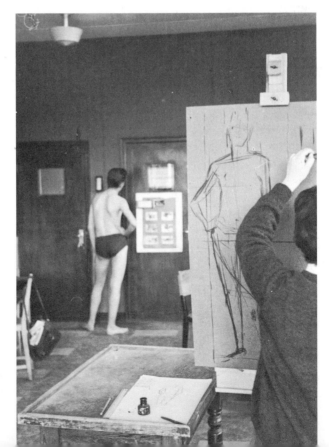

Fig. 61 Drawing the figure

Fig. 62 Figure study. Girl aged 16

The teacher may feel he can present certain experiences in such a way as to bring them more within reach. For example, the interest could be in landscape depth – a very common one at this time. Is there a place nearby with fairly strong features that show differences in size – as in near and far buildings, or directions of line seen in ploughland, sidewalks, bridge spans, or really noticeable colour and tone changes . . . perhaps even with irregular formations that allow small inaccuracies to be absorbed without upsetting the general effect and where strict definition can relax a little? Which of these give any individual student his clue to depth can only be

Fig. 63 Boy aged 14

known once he starts: it may be the relative sizes, the line directions, the colour and tone changes, a combination or none of these. It is a mistake to try and anticipate this by pointing to one set of clues. The old linear-perspective theory, for example, is a trap – a grid set up outside the true experience: it is passively adopted and used for evermore as a framework on which to hang observation. Feeling vanishes through it. In an outdoor situation set up to invite depth study, some students tackled it as a problem of line perspective (fig. 64), others discovered a depth statement within that set-up (fig. 63).

Fig. 64 Perspective. Boy aged 14

Fig. 65 Inside a clock. Boy aged 14

Preconceptions about a view get in the way of seeing it as it is at the moment. Taking up an unaccustomed position can help in seeing it in a fresh way – from low on the ground or high up, from under a railway bridge or a flight of steps, or from among standing machinery or vehicles.

An indoor lesson could enquire into the quality of surfaces, or into the intricate design of a precision instrument. In the first example, the teacher can arrange a contrast of objects (coarse, smooth, pitted, corrugated and so on) in a light that emphasizes their relationships and textures; the students should be able to handle the objects and explore different media in expressing them. In the second example, the precision instrument, work could quickly take over from assembling or dismantling it; from focusing on a part and enlarging it; or from imagining it as machinery in an invented situation: 'Inside a Clock' could just as well be 'Inside a Space-time Machine': the research and recording is there, yet the conception develops more personally. In fig. 65 this worked out in modelled paper and scrap.

As in the case of figures, groups of objects could form in a number of ways: in their own natural setting, e.g. pots by the kiln waiting to be fired; as a collection of contrasts; as having something in common, e.g. reflectiveness or weathering; having a 'family connection', e.g. all concerned with a particular trade; as being incongruous together. Such groupings are arbitrary and will

82

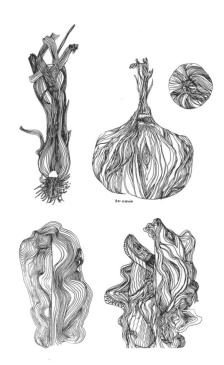

Fig. 66 Girls aged 14

inevitably overlap. The teacher may decide on the nature of the grouping, or the students' choice could be a better starting point for enquiry.

But the student's choice may not always be a safe guide. A boy who is passionate about motor cycles, for example, may find his mechanical knowledge leaves him dissatisfied with anything he can say about them visually. He may not be able to get past his own diagrams to make a more personal statement. Perhaps the teacher should draw him into experiences that are less central to him, but yet leave him with greater freedom of expression. Other intentions can take over from these studies at any stage if they are felt to lead in a new direction; for example, an examination of unlikely objects seen side by side might open the way to a 'nightmare' picture, or to ideas for design in fabric and embroidery and three-dimensional pieces.

The student's greater awareness generally leads him to look at things in more detail, and this takes on a significance in itself. Shapes, textures, colours, all begin to intrigue for their own sake. He may be carried away by these discoveries and confine his efforts to trying to explain them: a single feature of a landscape, details of a figure or animal, an isolated object. In fig. 66, students have been doing this in their study of different onions, and have used line drawing to follow the irregular texturing. In fig. 67, a student has been using dot-arrangements to do the same with leaves and

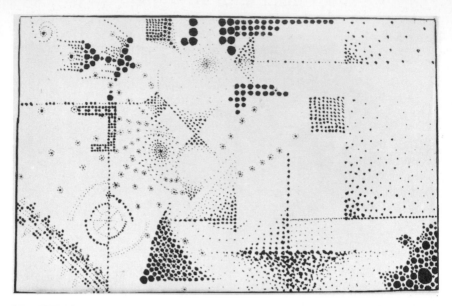

Fig. 67 Girl aged 16

insects. It is part of his growing understanding and may only later be absorbed more broadly. Time and again he will probably want to explore in this way. It could even happen that he discovers real creative possibilities within the detail, as with the intricacies of design in a crazed pottery glaze or imagined pictures in the flaking of rusted metal. He will only want helping over them if they hold him back too long from fuller statements.

Despite all this, there is the likelihood of a student becoming over-concerned with naturalistic aims and finding other responses falling away. The teacher can direct the strictly visual study into others of a different kind: a study of flower forms into one associating with flowers – a festival, a botanical adventure, jungles, love tokens, flower fantasies and symbolism; or the study of a stuffed owl into one of barns and lofts and midnight trees, or of the mysteries of night vision. The aim throughout is to deepen the responses at any level.

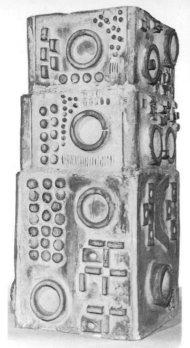

Fig. 68 **a,b** Plaster-cast slab sculpture and a painted relief Boys, girls, aged 15 to 17

Further media

Experiments with materials and processes continue during these years, but a student who has had fairly wide practice will probably prefer to be working with a chosen few. A familiar process can be reassuring when ideas are unsettled, and it would be sensible to consolidate any special abilities that have emerged. A student who has confidence in a few media will be likely to use them more expressively than if he were experimenting too widely. If he is unexpressive in a narrow range, or is just repetitive, he should be encouraged to venture beyond it; for example, a use of line limited to drawing on flat surfaces might extend to constructions with line in space, using wire or thread or cane. This is a good time for combining materials and processes, e.g. embroidery with puppet making, photography with construction.

New materials and processes that might start to appear now:

1 Further drawing and painting media such as pastels, oil pastels, polymer, acrylic and oil paint (fig. 69).
2 An increased range of materials for collage, mounted reliefs, mosaics and constructions (figs. 48, 68, 70).
3 Pottery processes – thrown, modelled, composite structures, kiln building (figs. 71, 72).
4 Modelling processes using different clays, plasters, wax, glass fibre with filler and laminating resin; casting in plaster, ciment fondu (u.s. ccment mix) or glass fibre and resin from moulds of plaster, paraffin wax or flexible synthetic materials – designing for a valid cast-effect rather than an inert duplication of the original form (figs. 74–77).

85

Fig 69

Fig 70

Fig. 69 Images that came from experiments with thick impasto paint. Girl aged 15
Fig. 70 Wall relief, using a bicycle wheel, plastic beakers and other scrap. Boys aged 15

5 Carving with harder woods such as pear, oak, yew, cherry, sycamore, maple, walnut, mahogany, teak; and with harder stone such as granite and alabaster.

6 Sculpture in metals, using soldering, brazing or welding processes (fig. 79).

7 Printmaking with larger blocks or more over-printing, and by other engraved or etched processes (with care needed if gravers or acids are used): 'accidental' pull-off effects resulting from the printing can now be better assimilated and used. In fig. 78, a painting has developed from the 'accident' of blot printing. Variations of screen printing on paper or fabric lengths.

8 Further work with other crafts introduced earlier (page 56) and with plastics, coloured glass, or other materials the teacher feels he can manage.

A process may develop scale or ingenuity through combining it with others. Experiments should grow from the student's need to extend what he is saying, and technical innovation should not be allowed to over-run them.

A further change in attitude is apparent about this time. Whereas, before, the student may have lost himself completely in the activity itself, the end-product is now becoming more important. He needs to feel he has done what he set out to do and that other people will like it. This striving to produce acceptable work can lead him to results quite unlike what he visualized or what he can really do.

Fig 71 A simple sawdust kiln. Inspecting the state of the firing

Fig. 72 A first experimental kiln using builder's scrap. This successfully fires biscuit ware

Fig. 73 Reflections. Girl aged 15

Fig. 74 Terracotta group. Boy aged 16

Fig. 75 Sculpture in plaster. Boys aged 14

F

Fig. 76 Plaster flow over a balloon. The experience with the material leads to discoveries of light and shadow effects when the balloon is pricked. Boy aged 15

Fig. 77 Wire, fabric and plaster sculpture. Girl aged 15

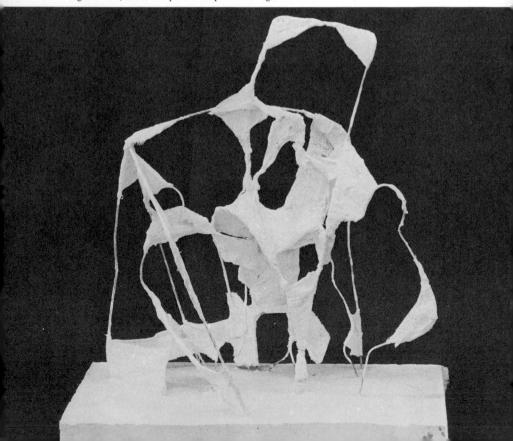

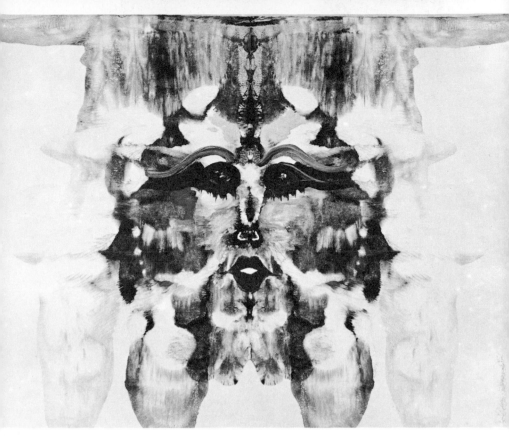

Fig. 78 Developing a 'blot' print. Girl aged 14

Fig. 79 Welded metal sculpture from flower forms. Boy aged 14

But overall, he is probably beginning to trust his judgment more and is not so dependent on others. What he achieves in these years depends largely on how far he can find a style of his own. It is through the confidence this gives him that he can begin to value what he does. The strengthening of style is nearly always a matter between the student and the teacher: over a period of time, a particular treatment of subjects or use of materials will probably be noticeable and will begin to mark out a personal way of working.

How much time for art?
As the student moves up the school, the time for art increases or decreases according to whether it has become a main subject or not. The value a school attaches to art also affects the allocation of time. A student with art as a main subject can either deepen it in certain areas, or broaden it across a number of areas. Any course, leading perhaps to examinations, should allow him to do either at any time and recognize all resulting work (easier with some Examination Boards than others!).

The student is probably with a smaller group by this time, even in some cases on his own. This again gives him more chance to expand, though he may have to fit in alongside a larger group from elsewhere in the school and carry on against the background of their activities. This is often the position where there is a very full art timetable and not enough room or staff. There can be an advantage in this in that both sides see what the other is doing and exchange ideas from time to time. Age differences do not matter. For most students, however, there will almost certainly be less time for art: they are more committed in other subjects. There may also be longer intervals between art periods. This all means that work has to be planned to make best use of the reduced time and to bridge the longer absences, unless an out-of-school programme is possible to restore the balance. The teacher may decide that only short-term projects should be attempted, those that can be completed in one or two sessions. If these are not to become just isolated experiences without time to develop any real meaning for the student, they should be directed, if only lightly, towards a longer term aim that gives them a sense of growth. It is quite possible, however, to plan for projects lasting over a number of weeks, even carried out in interrupted stages, if the intention can be sustained. In fact, a single project extending over a period can become a point of central interest for a student and one to which he returns with increasing pleasure as it develops. Care is needed naturally with materials that may deteriorate or become unworkable. During

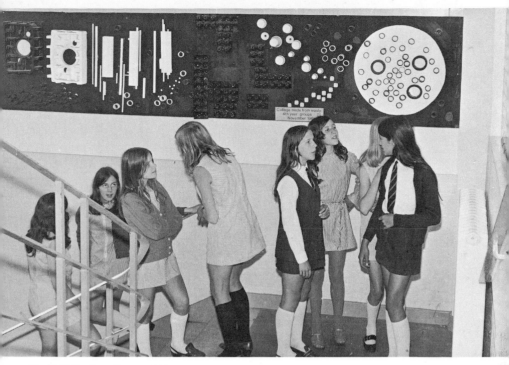

Fig. 80 Wall collage. Boys aged 15

this time art can contribute to other studies or provide a complete change from them, depending on what is needed most.

Group work
The group project still has its place in these years, but a student may not wish to see any contribution he makes merged with the rest to the extent that it loses its character. If he has come to value his finished work he will not willingly let parts go. Because of this, the group project tends to attract individual rather than communal efforts, where several students would have been working on the same piece; though the students will work together if they feel they have real responsibility for their own areas. If these have to be adapted later, it is better that this should be worked out early to avoid having to make big changes in them when they are nearly finished. The older student tends to adapt more flexibly. Fig. 80 shows a wall collage made from waste packing and other materials; there was a lot of give and take before final arrangement was decided on. Fig. 81 shows a plaster and mesh sculpture made by a group of older girls.

The group occasion may be one of the few where a student can join in work on any scale; and it is sometimes necessary for him to be involved in work bigger than himself. It may also be one of

Fig. 81 Plaster and mesh sculpture. Girls aged 16/17

Fig. 82 A problem of reflections

the few times when the students come together from their other studies, and it can take on the nature of a social event, arousing a certain ribaldry and protest that they would restrain if they were working on their own. No matter how little time a student can spend in the art room, he should feel he can go there whenever possible and keep up with any interests he has.

When creating stops
The student of this age can often dry up creatively, even under skilled guidance. The teacher may find he can introduce a different kind of experience to lessen the need for making creative decisions. Some of the following will be of use from time to time:
1 Sensory experiments using devices to note reactions, e.g. colour mixing with light – colour gelatines or cellophane cut to overlap in various combinations and fixed in a slide-mount to throw onto a screen; colour mixing with pigments – controlled tests with different opaque and transparent media; image or colour response to various sounds, scents, taste and touch, e.g. to a flute or running water, tar or lavender, a mint or a lemon, ice-cubes or a wire brush. Apparatus can be made to illustrate phenomena such as reflections, light and shadow effects, directions and movements in space or on a plane, buoyancy of forms and so on. In fig. 82, a number of objects have been assembled to illustrate different kinds of reflection. A similar experience was taken up later by a student to make a sculpture in aluminium and perspex (U.S. plexiglass), fig. 73, using the reflective quality of these materials, and a painting, fig. 83.

95

Fig. 83 Girl aged 17

2 Further visits to the works of artists and craftsmen (page 63).
The visits can be supported by film and slides and by any discussion arising from them. With the teacher's guidance, the
students may question how the various works came to be done
in the form they were – the motives behind them (commercial,
religious, civic, tribal, ideological, hierarchic, hallucinatory, and
so on). In understanding their origins, attempts at imitation can
be seen as meaningless and with no validity for the student in
his own times and work.
3 Research into different art media – their origin, nature, uses and
history, together with physical and emotional reactions to them.
4 Linking art studies with studies of other kinds (page 99).
These studies should encourage the collection of illustrative material
and comment in folio form for organizing impressions and ideas.

Time on their hands
One aspect of these later years stands out – some teachers might say that it gives them more headaches and heart-searching than any other – the student who is only waiting to finish with school and get out to a job. Every day is a waste of time and he openly resents it. As far as he is concerned, he is just marking time until the moment he can be off. Schools are trying to face this with more vocational courses, with modified examination incentives, and with release-arrangements that let a student spend some of his time with a trade or concern outside. But apart from students who may be involved in these, many feel there is no point in staying on at all. They look on the art lesson and most others as a bore, as time-off, or merely as a golden opportunity to liven things up.

I have already expressed a personal feeling that no teacher (art or any other) should have to exhaust himself in finding ways of occupying students against any chance of their gaining from his subject. The teacher has enough to do without having to scratch around for the odd grain of interest that might attract them. At the same time, the students should not be left to wilt in this condition. The condition brightens if work in the school is seen more and more to come from a personal responsibility for whatever is done; and with such a tradition behind them, many more students, by the time they reach the leaving stage, will have come to look forward to their remaining opportunities in the art room. Until such a tradition builds up, and while the present conditions last, there will still be teachers and students in this uneasy relationship with each other.

Over the school as a whole, with several subjects concerned, a solution might lie in letting teenagers get together over similar interests – scooters, records, wrestling, make-up, films and so on – with timetabling for any staff who could lend their own skills to this. In many present instances, this would be no more than bringing certain out-of-schools activities into the day's programme. It could happen that a student, released from having to do art, would return to it from choice as time went on.

Teachers may have other means of dealing with the situation in their school, e.g. an organized service in the district, but most will be left with the problem in their own room. What can the art teacher do until matters improve? The following are a few suggestions by way of compromise.
1 Visits to places outside the school where productive work is going on (this is the adult world, and can attract for that reason): a factory, an assembly plant, a printing works, a tannery, a mason's yard, a furniture workshop, a fashion house, a forge, a

shipyard, a paint or cosmetics manufacturer, a pottery, a building site, restoration work, road and bridge building schemes. The help of a specialist from the place concerned will usually add spice to the visit. He can explain better what is happening and give the visit a sense of occasion.

2 Constructive work that may need doing around the art room, e.g. fixing and surfacing a display area, shelves, etc., building a kiln or puppet theatre, preparing stage properties and sets, devising and making apparatus or lesson aids. Jobs calling for mechanical or electrical skills, like stage lighting, may provide an opening for certain students and keep them within a creative field (boys who fix the stage lighting are drawn in some way into the drama situation).

3 Activities with a social or more sophisticated appeal, e.g. film making: the nature of the group would suggest the best approach – documentary, dramatic, animated, sound, silent; photography – taking film, processing, enlarging, mounting, making slides, experimental work; printing – type setting, printing work for the school or a social group outside: even a small handprinting machine can be absorbing. These are just examples. The teacher will discover others. If they are planned not just as time-fillers but as being worthwhile in themselves, they can do much to make these last months happy ones.

6   Sources in other subjects

It is for convenience only that we give art a name, but by doing so, we can come to think of it as an activity apart from other ones, and as having rules and special times and places in the week for doing it. How can art be felt as a way into and out of a wider sense of experience? In a flexibly ordered environment such as we find in the first years in some primary schools, this happens naturally, with interests falling away and reforming continuously as the day goes on (with art among them). Though we might hope this could happen at all levels, it is not the position we have at the moment in most secondary schools. The secondary school as we know it is an environment of separate disciplines, partly from choice, partly from pressures. It is administered largely to sustain an expected pattern of attainment, and in such a way as to measure this, i.e. by subjects. It is, by this device and by the habits of acceptance it inspires among the greater number, competitive. This is a pressure, right or wrong, which prolongs sub-division within the school. The best efforts to change this come up against the demands of external examinations, of inadequate buildings, impossible numbers, and conflicting attitudes. But still the only progress that will be made is by the individual teachers within a school agreeing some means by which the student can think and move more naturally across their various areas. It is mainly a matter of background planning and subject co-operation. The idea of a planned integration of subjects where two or more combine their approaches to a theme can form up into just another compartment unless it keeps its aims very relaxed. The association could be quite an unnatural one for a student, and the connection between the studies unreal. Subjects in harness tend to plough the same furrow. I believe that the artificial linking of art with other subjects is in danger of merely enlarging its separateness.

The merging of interests is more an *attitude* to be developed across the school, encouraging ideas to root and grow in areas where they do so naturally and where the soil is right. 'But' (there will be an outcry), 'even if we wanted to, we couldn't do it. We have our timetable, and other teachers have theirs. We have students for an hour here, an hour there, and then they go off and more students arrive to take their place. We are tied. What can we do? We must accept the position as it is.' What *can* we do? What can the art teacher do from his particular place in the school?

First, the teaching in the art room can, by its variety, give the student broad freedoms to explore. Discoveries do not necessarily show. As long as the teacher feels that discoveries and experiments are taking place he need not worry that they are not on the surface where he can see them. Time may show where they have led.

a   b

Fig. 84a Machining at school. Girl aged 11
    b Machining at home. Girl aged 11

But supposing a student is really stuck? Supposing he can find no starting point? A possible one might lie in an interest elsewhere that he does not necessarily associate with art: it could open unexpectedly onto expressive work – and the teacher may be able to help. To do so, he would need to keep in mind a picture of what is being done in other subject areas, so that he could follow up any possible ways in which they could connect for the student. Where might the connections lie?

Domestic and practical crafts
The domestic subjects touch home ground – the student's own and others' homes. A whole concept of life in the home – a refuge, a battleground, a place for privacy and for private disclosures – may be thrown into relief for a student by experience with a school oven and recipes, or furnishings, clothes, a sewing machine, room decoration or baby care. Comparisons are inevitable. She is making judgments, and reacting in some way. Can she bring something of this into the open? Can she express what she may be feeling but could not say elsewhere? There may be nothing; or there may be thoughts she would be relieved to express . . . perhaps away from where they

100

Fig. 85 Embroidery. **a** Girl aged 17
    b Girl aged 12

a   b

centre . . . perhaps in the art room (figs. 84 a,b).

She may have been looking at the history of costume. Is there a big decorative painting or collage somewhere in the air, or an appliqué figure, or rubbings? Or just a chance to fall in love with fans and parasols, brooches and cameos and period portraits? Maybe to imagine and make one of her own?

Sewing and machining skills and a feel for fabrics lead into new embroideries, appliqué, drama costumes, constructions – perhaps with other materials. Figs. 85 a,b illustrate uses of these skills in making an embroidery, and a fabric picture.

There is probably a woodwork area in the school, and one for metalwork – maybe one for special work in other crafts: spinning and weaving, basketry, building. The student may have found a home in one of these, getting to know the materials well, doing more with them. What he does there may find new scope in the art room. A feeling for wood, shaping in his hands to a stool or bowl, is the same feeling that could carve a newly imagined form, or build structures for a new idea. A feeling for metal that he has shaped and forged in the metal workshop could also shape a sculpture in metals. These are starting points that are familiar! (Figs. 86, 87). They may help again and again in general ways as

101

Fig. 86   Fig. 87

Fig. 86 Experience in shaping wood leads to sculpture. Boy aged 18
Fig. 87 Blocking out with saw and gouges. Boy aged 13

Fig. 88 Sculpture in tubes, using polypropane rainwater pipes and perspex (plexiglass), from studies of
machines made in Technical Drawing. Boy aged 16

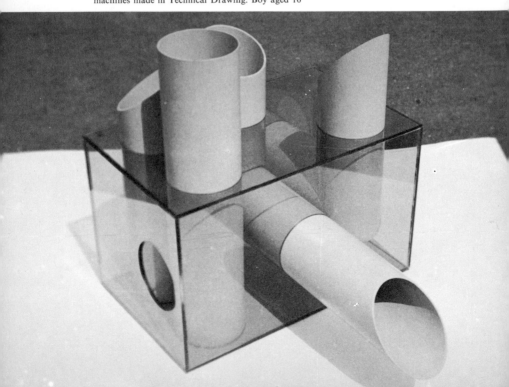

well: assembling and securing constructions, making armatures and other supports, producing special tools or apparatus he needs.

Skills with yarn, cane, fibreglass, cement and other materials all lead to further work at other levels of invention.

Drama

The play holds life for a while, watches it, feels for it, makes incidents sharper and relationships clearer, exaggerates gesture and expression, has a sense of occasion: the ritual, direction, costume, lights and sound. The spectator is drawn in or repelled; the actor is *in* it, involved, identifying with it. Has the student been involved? The spell of the play is strong: it may be so for him, and images from it inspire him to give them another shape. The process has already begun: there are scenes set as he remembers or imagines them, and actors ready to step in. They may already be almost a picture, a model, a puppet play as they are. Only paint is needed, or what will make models and puppets.

What was the scene? 'The Arrival of a Guest', 'An Approaching Storm', 'Death on a Summer's Morning'? Is a painting far away? Was the student 'waiting for the guest' or was he 'the guest'? The versions will be different. How did everyone know there was a storm coming? How did they show it? What was it that died on a summer's morning, and how did everyone feel about it? Are there paintings or work of other kinds here? Did he go to a theatre? Was this the real occasion for him: the atmosphere, the darkening and lightening, the audience, everyone watching the same thing, disengaging from it? Perhaps the theatre was outdoors: sky, trees, a town park, a ruined castle. Was everything else around more real or less real because of it?

The long history of the theatre too – has he been looking back through it: the miracle plays, masques, high drama, pageants; the staging, the manners, the sets and costumes, the ornate or makeshift auditoriums, the playbills and posters, the travelling theatre, the theatre of other nations? In fig. 89 a student's interest in old theatre mask illustrations has led her to carve a plaster relief from one.

The practical associations with drama in the school are renewed with each school production: building sets and properties, dressing and making-up, colours of lighting, arresting notices. Could the play and the art grow together, developing ideas from either side right through rehearsals, improvising adjustments between the action and the set until they arrive at an agreed form for the final production?

103

Fig. 89 Girl aged 17

Fig. 90 Girl aged 15

Fig. 91 Contour study. Boy aged 15

Geography

What does the study of this subject entail: exploring the land and skies and oceans, their deep movements and rest, the forces at work in them, their waste and abundance, their zones of survival and defeat? Does it follow rivers and descend mines? And read the signs of a past world that died for this one? Probably to a student of the subject quarries, clouds and dunes are already vivid, and will come to life for him through the materials available in the art room. His feeling for the action that carved fjords, compiled coral, lifted a continent up slowly, could be something to say in his art. Where could it start: on paper on the floor with a wash of sea colour from one side, and a wash of shore colour from the other, meeting as the sea and shore meet; or on a board with plaster or modelled paper becoming canyons and causeways, islanded fens or the long roll of the Atlantic; as fine wires stretched across space, tracing the skeins of wind and currents and bird migration; as glitter on glass, laying down an arctic; as clay, hollowing the journey into caves? In fig. 90 the inspiration of land forms has found expression through paper modelling and ink design. Fig. 91 is a card relief from studies in contour geography.

Has the weather carved exposed ridges? Can stone be carved in the same way? What have other artists done with high-pressure air hoses? Has history walked through pitch and ice, settled in amber, left footprints in hardening rock, drowned near coasts? Does it happen again like this for the imagination in a picture or a new shape? What are the earth and sea made of: clay, stone, slate, chalk, sand, fibres, reeds, cane, coal, colours? How have they been used by the people living among them: sculpture from paper, masks from forest woods, amulets and tools from bone, paintings from prehistoric earths and irons? Our ancestors charted their world with monsters and mermaids and elaborate signs and symbols: are there ideas for original design?

History and social studies

Where is the student among the pages of the past? What is his sense of being there, of being in it as it goes on? Does he feel himself involved, or a spectator? Can he get close to the events and the schemings and the ideas? Can he assemble them in pictures, enact them in clay, build them from anything? Would he scale the Heights of Abraham in a wall collage or chisel a cement block with some of the hazards of ascent he feels? Would he find uniforms and weapons in appliqué or puppetry? Would the Armada meet Drake with more gusto in a painting, or the *Santa Maria* moor

105

in the Indies in embroidery? Can medieval knights be armoured in can-metal sculpture or foil reliefs, and their ladies dressed in glass mosaic? The Gold Rush, the building of thè pyramids, the finding of a lost explorer, or radium, or a trail across the young America may all come to him in the art room. Fig. 92 shows a model that a group of students made, inspired by their interest in the life of a medieval village. A sense of the past can create any 'cowboy' or 'pirate'; 'sunrise' can be imagined over Stonehenge or over Easter Island; embroidery can spring from the vaulting traceries of an old cathedral, or a mobile float from the voyages of the first balloons.

Life as it happened – how did artists see it and craftsmen give it its everyday shape? There are portraits to meet, monuments in stone and bronze and brass, manuscripts, the tools of the farmer and the mariner, fashions of transport, homes, life outdoors, devices of war, cities and suburbs that grew and faded – or go on growing? In figs. 93a, b, c students have constructed buildings from past and present, using card, balsa wood, straw, perspex, cement block and polystyrene (U.S. styrofoam). What did races make of each other when they raided, visited, settled? What was a carved canoe to Darwin and to Captain Cook (life or death?), or the New Amsterdam waterfront to a settler from a Devon village?

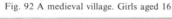

Fig. 92 A medieval village. Girls aged 16

Fig. 93a,b Buildings from different times. Constructions in card, balsa wood, straw, perspex (plexiglass), cement block and polystyrene (styrofoam). Boys, girls aged 13 to 15

b

Fig. 94 School Magazine

LD AGE

is my opinion that old age pensioners are not given the treatment and respect from our society nich they deserve. The only function seemingly allocated to them in our society is as a political nnis ball. In as much as a great deal of notice is taken of them during the game, after it they are cked away and forgotten until the next match.

bygone and uncivilized societies the elderly were much respected, and served their societies as eful councillers to the young. Not like our technocratical society which looks on them as a burden, t a blessing.

iey are looked on as social outcasts, for after retirement they are expected to disappear, by a society eamlined to the under thirty-fives. After retirement from industry and involuntary retirement from ciety they are looked after by a variety of pensions at pittance level and if they want, National surance also, on which most survive on a subsistance level.

i the whole pensioners have little money, poor housing and the smallest amount of food to keep emselves from starving. Many of these pensioners are forced by relatives into old pensioners homes, ich instead of helping, often rob these people of their last interests in life, giving rise to mental generation. In fact, many turn to vegetables, unable to fend for themselves.

is true, better housing and increase in pensions would be of great benefit to the pensioner, but this solving half the problem. For to solve this problem completely, they must be fitted back into our ciety, not as a burden, but as useful citizens, thus giving them a purpose in life.

e older people, with their patience and understanding, if listened to and taken heed of by the unger generation, could help to mellow our violent society. For I personally have found the advice my Grandparents invaluable in shaping my life. They have taught me the value of tolerance and an preciation of nature and life. This was not conveyed to me by word, but by watching them living ch day to its fullest, as if it was the last day they had to live. If more people tried to understand old people they might gain a greater appreciation of life.

Christopher Brice
Fifth Year

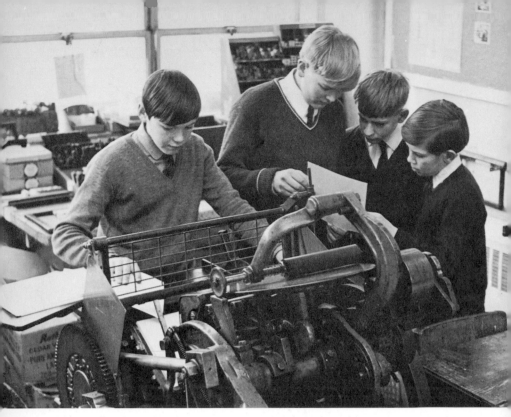

Fig. 95 Use of a school printing press is part of the overall creative activity. Work is printed for the school (magazine, notices, etc.) and for other schools whenever possible

Language

Language is full of seen images. Do stories and verse and plays have a special magic for the student? Perhaps not only these, but the words he plays with, struggles with, that are everywhere around him – words that startle and quieten, make labyrinths or bridges to other people, or to a new idea. Where is he among all the markets of language? Is there a book, a passage, a phrase, something he has said or heard that could move him towards a drawing or painting? What is a 'dark moon'? Is it hidden, masked, brilliant in a dark sky, brooding on a land black with shadows? Words suggest; will a picture or construction with a source of light take it further and touch the imagination at other levels?

Is there a tale that calls for characters; an astonishing description; an attempt at description that has failed with words but may succeed with colour ('What was it like on the big dipper at the fair last night?')? Was there a strange dream that certain objects could strangely reconstruct? There was the word 'DANGER' he saw; the newspaper report of 'Old people on their own'; a film title *It Came from the Sky*; an idea he had, 'I am blind and have never seen my mother'; the conversation of some girls he overheard . . . are there pictures here?

And there is all the vocabulary he knows that adults miss that may be full of images: shouts in a game, secrets, talk about boy and girl friends and sex. He may not repeat them aloud, but he

Fig. 96 A geometric design mounted in keeping with the wall surface pattern. Girls aged 13

might in a picture. And are there mysteries of other alphabets and unreadable scripts? Do they attract him like curious designs: hieroglyphics, newspapers in Hebrew or Turkish, signs in Chinese, archaic scrolls and tablets? What about the many faces of type he can identify, designed for special purposes: Garamond, Helvetica, Caslon? Do they all open doors to imaginary worlds or to the great commercial scene around him that feeds on words?

Mathematics
Does he think about space and relationships and what goes on around him – and measure them? What is he measuring at the moment: time, distance, sound, light, speed, growth? Is he asking questions with diagrams and finding answers with them, or with planes and calculable forms? Is he happiest with the rhythm and precision of number? Does he just like lines that will do the things they are told to – that he can manipulate? Could he bring this interest to other materials and find that they lift it into new experience, his thoughts taking colour, form and movement from them (fig. 96)? Solids made from paper have a different life in planes of translucent, coloured plastic. Pyramids lead straight to deserts and different suns, casting shadows for speculation. Figures of geometry can spin thread and fine wire across fixed points in space

111

or on a flat surface. The adventure of lines that intersect and radiate and touch can adventure further into curve stitching. Bodies that relate in weight and balance and direction to each other already hold the principle of mobiles. Mosaics deal in unit squares. Parabolas are at the heart of throwing stones, parallels at the heart of ploughland and cities, and crossing arcs at the heart of a pitching sea. Spirals are also whirlpools and stairways and snail shells. Most of mathematics can conjure with abstract shapes, flat or solid. Designs await.

What devices have been made for measuring: the abacus, ingenious clocks, sounding instruments, theodolites, sextants, signal apparatus, computors? What of their shapes and action? Do they hold ideas for design, for imaginative devices (a machine that measures silence, or feelings, or time in dreams)?

Music
Guitars, Zulu dance beat, Wagner, lullabys and blues, gentle sounds, passionate sounds, Bach original, Bach as jazz . . . is it all going on somewhere for the student who sits with a blank paper, an idle brush, and a black hour of art ahead? Has he left elsewhere another part of himself, something that could make him dive for paints, fill the paper, or feel for its forms in clay and stone, its patterns in mosaic? Somewhere he may be able to start with music – music he makes, dances to, listens to; the sounds and rhythms of it; the images, moods, sensations. As melody moves lightly over strings, colour can wash a surface; as brass urges, and voices mass, and one flute comes softly in, so paint can . . . tones . . . impasto . . . brushwork. The feeling is for a new medium, but seen now, not heard. The picture builds up, the clay or the wood forms, gauzes and sequins and lace compose. There is a memory of music in them. Did the music happen somewhere outside the school, in a recent music lesson, just now in the art room? Has it left images for the student that could pass into colour or form? Is the music happening at this moment (a tape or record or radio playing)? Can a brush follow its calm or energy, its gay or grave measures, its rise and fall and rests as they occur? The paintings in fig. 97 were done to different kinds of music:

(a) Beethoven's Symphony No. 5
(b) Coming thro' the rye
(c) Strawberry Fair
(d) Fingal's Cave
(e) The Blue Danube
(f) John Brown's Body.

112

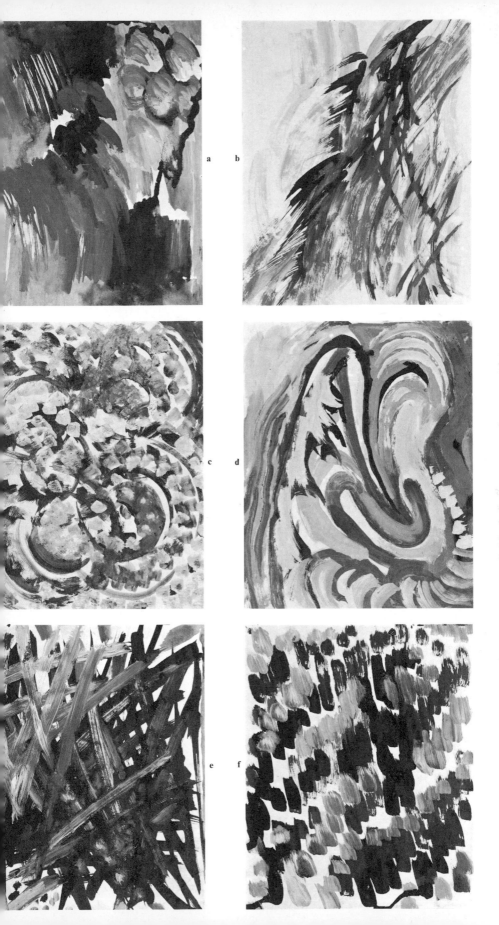

a   b

c   d

e   f

Fig. 98 Pop session. Girls aged 18

Fig. 99 Wood engraving. Boy aged 14

Fig. 100 Girl aged 17

Fig. 98 is a painting made after a session of pop music.

Has an opera or musical left scenes and characters he could recall – perhaps expansively (they were larger than life) in a wall
collage or in group puppetry? Were there dance forms that could
flow into brush drawing or into flexible wire and cane and reed,
or into clay? Are there instruments he has studied (used perhaps)
from other times and countries? Do designs lie in their shapes and
action? Or in the symbols of scoring and notation? Players and
performers may be a subject. The wood engraving in fig. 99 is from
the idea of a street musician. The plaster carving in fig. 100 developed from an intuitive connection between the block shapes and the
shapes of the organ and the organist. Fig. 101 is of a pop group to
which the student belongs.

Fig. 101 Boy aged 16

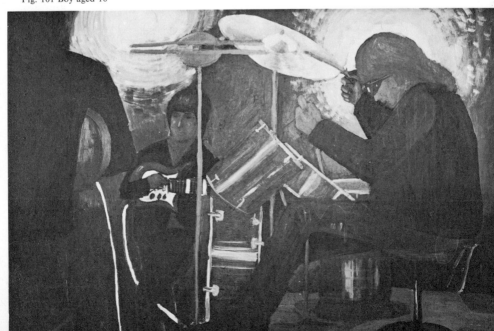

Fig. 102 Child Buddha. Girl aged 17   Fig. 103 Prophet. Boy aged 15

Religious studies

Sources of inspiration are at all depths of belief and disbelief. The student may be at any one of them and want to express it: the questions of origin, direction, ends; the outward forms of practice. What does he believe as a result of background and family observance, from thinking things out for himself, from a conversion experience? Has something become important, reassuring, disturbing, angering? Will brushes help, or charcoal, chisels, spatulas? Where does it start for him: in himself; in what he watches or takes part in: assemblies, marches, bands, demonstrations, witness meetings, missions, action groups, pilgrimages, ritual; in what he learns about: religious wars, settlements, personalities, other gods, ancient faiths, symbolism? Fig. 102 is from the story of Buddha. Interest for the student focused in the shape of the child Buddha suggested by the plaster block. In fig. 103 a student has carved in stone his impression of an Old Testament prophet.

What have artists in other times and places said in their religious work or made for their religion in painting, sculpture, architecture, illumination, stained glass, mosaics, devotional objects, church furniture? Why did they do it that way? Because of their faith, influences or pressures on them, materials available?

Does the student's own place of worship mean a lot to him? Can he get inspiration from it?

116

Science

The student is now interested in the way things grow and work, in the nature of what they are. The interest could have a strong hold on him. Can he take his searches and discoveries further through his art, expressing more personally what he knows and wonders about? He may need a chance to do this. Science has brought him so far: has he his own way of seeing apart from this? He has met pulleys and prisms, hibernation and seed dispersal, coal gas and iodine. The evidence is building up: facts are being agreed. What are they to him on other levels? Do they open into another kind of imagination or invention, into his own responses more, into interpretations beyond science – ones that are real, but only for himself, not for proving? Fig. 104 is a sculpture in polypropane pipe off-cuts based on the universal joint of a car and compass. Figs. 105 107 illustrate sculptures arising from investigations into seed-forming (the fir cone, poppy heads, etc.). The materials used here include perspex, metal foil and acetate sheet. He may have been studying the potato: its germination, cell structure, content, food value, diseases and so on. Does he want to explore its grotesque shapes, the journey he pictures for it underground as it puts out shoots, the montage of its foliage, the paper sculpture of its flower, or (under a microscope perhaps) the modelled moon-craters of its 'eyes'?

Fig. 104 Boy aged 17

Fig. 105 Sculpture studies in 'seed forms. Boys, girls aged 17

Fig. 106   Fig. 107

Are other discoveries in the air: light, colour, magnetic fields, sound waves, space, organisms, chemical associations, time, the atom, science fiction and ancient sciences that seem like fiction? Anywhere here there may be ideas that he could develop, fantasies that arise from his studies ('Battle of air-borne seeds over the last garden in the city'); experiences he could stage from what he has learned (a mosaic or collage from the sound-vibration pattern of metal filings); mysteries he could linger over (creation theories flock to paint and floating structures). Did science look at the mechanics of flight: thistledown, bats, dragonflies? Could he, in his art, look at other dragons and dreams of flying; or make things that fly? Fig. 109 is a model in unfired clay and light alloy mesh based on the story of Icarus.

What does he know of the instruments of science? Are there designs and new forms among their complex shapes and action? Gases and liquids in motion may spill (outside the laboratory only) into imagined scenes of holocaust or strange dreams. What might there be, once the chance is taken? Fig. 110 is one of several experiments carried out by a student from such experiences. In this, he used perspex (u.s. plexiglass), metal and nylon tights to create a new structure based on what he had been doing in physics.

118

Fig. 108 Construction in strawboard from studies of the skull and with the invention of 'thought cavities'. Girl aged 17

Fig. 109 Boy aged 16

Fig. 110 Boy aged 18

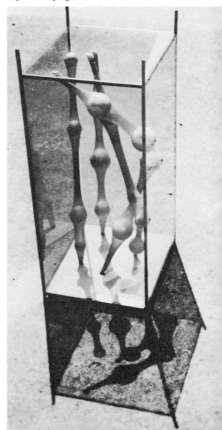

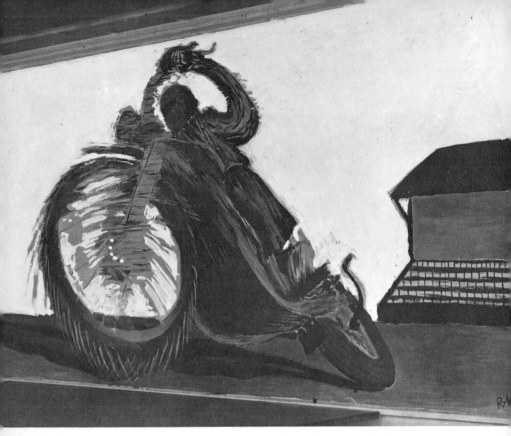

Fig. 111 Wall painting, from an interest in motor-cycle speedway. Boy aged 15

Fig. 112 Wall painting, street games. Girls aged 15

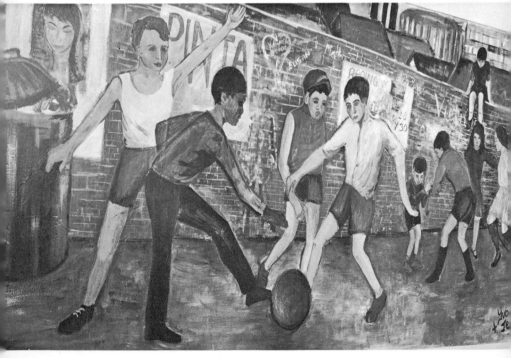

120

Sport and athletics

The quick manoeuvre on the field, the mounting tension, the effort
on the track, the timing of a dive, the return of a service, the thrills
and spills and daring chances . . . are these what the student is
really thinking about? Does he dream back to them and forward to
them next time? Are there actions here, ready to hand, for modelling
in clay or wire or shadow puppets? He knows the movements: he
can feel them in his body. He has shared in the emotion and suspense
on pitches and courts, in packed stadiums and school gymnasiums.
Could he express them? He expresses better what he knows (fig.
111).

He has played in a team: could he be one of a team in the art
room, working out a game together as a large painting or a sculptural
project? Attitudes, conflicts, decisions, they all come into it (fig.
112).

Perhaps he has studied the history of sports and knows about
hawking, jousting, circus races, ancient Olympics. Has he collected
emblems, trophies, badges, shields, insignia of all sorts connected
with them? Do they suggest original experiments in design, or
bring past scenes to mind?

Staff may be able to fit in visits to each others' rooms to bring fresh
ideas to bear on what is being done. The geography teacher might
be willing to talk from his special knowledge about pottery clays
and minerals, or about different kinds of stone used in carving;
other teachers might talk about the nature and performance of
woods, metals, plastics; about the principles of windmills and
diving bells; about the construction of musical instruments. And
people's hobbies sometimes cut right across the subjects they teach.

There are times when a number of subjects work together, pooling
the various skills, as in drama, film making, an environmental
search, a debate, producing a school journal or pageant. They all
serve to bring ideas and activities within a common aim, and
broaden understanding throughout the school.

H

7 Assessment and marking

It is clear that a student's creative work cannot be judged as roses or street lighting would be judged. I am talking about work that comes from the adolescent's own experience, not work that has been 'performed' to follow prescribed lines. This should concern us only to the extent of seeing that we do not encourage it. The value that a piece of work has for the adolescent is its value for *him*. How we react does not affect this, except in the way we apply an arbitrary scale of comparison. It has no real meaning for him against such a scale. We can judge how much the work moves us, or fails to do so, and the adolescent will undoubtedly be affected by this one way or the other. But what he put into it or got out of it may not show, certainly on the outside. He may have succeeded or failed in a way we do not see. Our reaction measures what we expect as much as our understanding of him. We encourage the student to express what he sees and feels and imagines: for the result to be weighed against how it ought to be, is to make nonsense of the aim and leave lengthening doubts in the student's mind. He will move towards what he thinks is expected of him – towards some acceptable attainment and into safe, highly-marked areas where this is possible. This is the danger: not just that marking must assume a particular target to be reached, but that it involves all those who are concerned with other targets.

The educational air is electrified with expectations of visible progress. Experience is not enough in itself apparently: it must be shown to have happened, shown to have a shape. It must be defined, communicated – forgetting that its value may lie outside any attempt to demonstrate it. So the teacher has a scale of judgment ready to hand, graduated according to his own sensibilities and to a standard agreed or fashionable among others. All this does is to assess the result of the pressures the system applies. The art teacher finds himself, along with most teachers and with the students, caught up in this attitude – not always directly, in the sense of having to give 'percentage credit' for work (though this lingers peacefully on), but in the sense that almost instinctively he is having to balance one kind of achievement against another all the time, and sift it into a category because art too must be in the general shuffle. The students expect it because they have come to think of ability ratings in art and that these should count in any overall rating.

So, must we stand by while the system grinds on? I do not think so. The art teacher should stand out against the whole idea of marking, making his claim ultimately on behalf of students everywhere for the simple creative freedoms. Meanwhile, he must continue to assess the students as he sees best, that is, in a way that can help them. He must try to keep the student and his work in focus

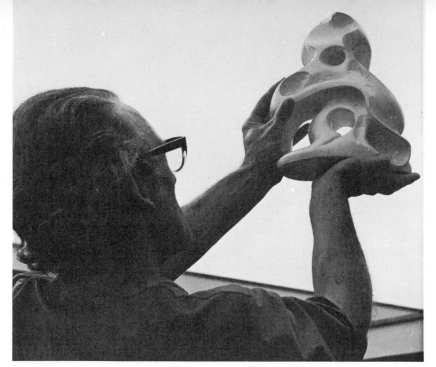

Fig. 113 Carving. Girl aged 14

together and build up a picture from what he knows of the student's hopes for the work and success with it. This is the first and only real reason for assessment, as a guide to his own thinking for the student's sake. If he is called upon to give an assessment for any other reason, it can only be on the basis of this, but he must do all he can to keep to a minimum any implied comparisons that are certain to be read into any such exercise.

It is worth questioning at this point whether 'assessment' is the right word to be using here. What the teacher is looking for is evidence of any development in the student's attitude and circumstances that may bring about changes in his work. How will the teacher interpret the evidence?

Among the first things he will look for is creative initiative – how naturally the student is moved to expression and how far he can sustain the initiative. He will give time for the results to show, and not try to anticipate them; expecting a certain kind of result could prejudice the outcome. What a student is trying to express may have meaning for him only in the way he presents it, and lead him to a use of line or colour or form that has little to do with any fixed ideas. He may be using tools and materials in the only way that will produce the effect he wants. Imagination must either invent its own means or subscribe to known ones that are less suitable. The teacher will also know how he himself is disposed towards what the student is doing and not let his judgment be over-coloured by this, though it would be unnatural for his feelings not to affect it in some way.

All this does not mean that every unrecognizable piece of work will have a value of its own (there will be reasons why it is so), but that it may be trying for something outside the recognized canons.

123

What the student does may be no more than an inhibited or nerveless attempt at conventional rendering; but one would like to be sure. Beyond this evidence of what the student achieves on his own, the teacher will notice what he does when he is working as one of a group. The same thoughts would apply. He may look for more particular evidence. How does the student interpret the experience (as he sees it, or feels for it, or thinks about it)? Is he imaginative? What materials does he choose and how well does he use them? Is his work derivative or copied at all? Let us look at this in more detail.

Interpretation

What a student repeatedly selects from his experiences indicates where his interest lies. He may be productive there: he may be trapped. His interpretation of subjects will probably show visual or other tendencies (see page 33). He may be treating them from outside, as an observer, or identifying more closely with them. In the same way, ideas and intuition will show: it is mostly a matter of emphasis. The real nature of his creativity may just be starting to appear, or it may have become clouded by other influences. Whichever is the case, the teacher should be guided by what the student finds most absorbing and does best. But it is easy to attribute to a work qualities that the student never intended. The work may, for example, have qualities of boldness or abstraction that a maturer artist might envy. To single these out for praise could lead to confusion. The so-called 'qualities' could seem to the student a weakness. He could have been trying for a closer likeness and finer detail; and to have his 'failure' praised can throw him off-course. He might take little notice, but the approval it earned could prompt him to to go on repeating it against his own judgment and without conviction.

Imagination

Imagination in a work has something to do with the way the work can surprise. Somehow it has escaped the conventions, and seems to have come about without their help. And it convinces. There is a quality about it – maybe the idea, or how the idea is put across, or how the materials are used – a quality of being a new experience.

It could be that in a particular work this effect is no more than visual ignorance on the student's part, or a technical accident, the outcome being only an interesting mistake. An autumn tree that seems to float from the earth and join its leaves in flight through the air may have been meant to be securely anchored by its roots in a perfectly normal way; what appears an imaginative conception to the teacher could be nothing of the kind to the student. He may believe it *is* firmly rooted if he can not see his 'mistake' – or he may know it is wrong and be disappointed in the result. Similarly, accidental texturing in a print, due to under- or over-inking, could have an atmosphere the student never intended and would rather scrap than have rhapsodized over. How and when a teacher can usefully talk about these chance qualities will depend on the student's readiness to value them. But either way they help in the teacher's overall picture of him.

At its extreme, imagination is close to fantasy. Perhaps a student can step into and out of a fantasy world at will, and knows it for what it is. But again, the fantasy may be real for him in a fuller sense, replacing what is normally thought of as reality. Or fact and fantasy may not have resolved themselves and the edges dividing them still be blurred. It helps to know where the student stands if his work is to be read rightly – though getting to know this could take time, and several pictures.

Use of materials

This is central to any kind of assessment. Is the student content to use only a few materials and processes? If so, is it because he can say all he wants to through them, and say it well – or is it because he cannot bring himself to use others, even though his present ones are not getting him any further? The question is, how far and how well is the student using the materials he could be using? Just as he can be limited by restricting himself, so too he can be by attempting to range too widely if his various excursions into other media lack a direction within himself. Does something of his own personality carry across into whatever medium he turns to, so that each work is clearly his? If it does not, he is probably working without any real purpose. Linked with this, how is he managing with tools? He can only be judged in the handling of tools that he wants to use. With any others, it would be a false picture of his practical ability; but given right ones, the picture could change and his ability be judged better.

Work with others

Advances may be taking place less at a strictly personal level than on the more social one of learning to work with others. The advances can be just as real and just as important. Any success of this kind must be recognized for the achievement it is.

125

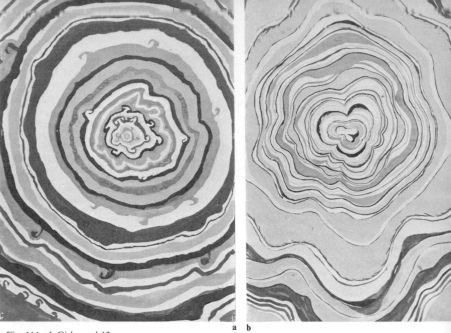

Fig. 114 **a,b** Girls aged 12

a   b

Copying

This may be no more than borrowing an idea from somewhere and converting it to new ends, or it may be a case of outright copying. In between, are the various degrees of imitation. Much of this is natural and could be of help: dead imitation seldom is. Figs. 114 a,b show paintings by two students who influenced each other but developed their work in their own way. How far a work is derivative may be obvious to a teacher knowing the student and his usual work, or the source from which he took it. Parts that have been copied are usually out of keeping with the rest and stand out fairly noticeably. Why copying happens is discussed elsewhere (page 13): there is probably a shift in the student's attitude, and this should concern the teacher more than the effect in any single piece of work.

The picture of an all-round attainment and sensibility as the aim of teaching is a misleading one. Big blind spots could be a handicap for the student, though on other sides he may be seeing well and strengthening a particular kind of vision. It is better that this should take place than that he should have to broaden his attempts to take in what is meaningless in order to satisfy a desirable balance. His work will almost certainly lose its character.

Advances are seldom startling. For most of the time they come about in small ways and in unexpected places, and break through almost unnoticed from earlier levels. Sometimes they are overwhelmed before the breakthrough can become established; so it is worth watching for them. The advance may be slight, but its value must lie in how happy the student feels about it. To overlook a small advance now may shorten the chance of a bigger one ahead: but to make too much of it could isolate it and set up secondary aims outside the real direction he was aiming for. The teacher can, however, help a student to recognize and consolidate any advance he makes.

126

8 The art room

The art room is an environment where ideas and materials continually reshape each other, and where related activities of all kinds can be carried on (film making, discussion, building stage sets and so on). What exactly this environment is, and how it comes about, is something more than its store of materials and tools. It has to do with these things, but it is in the way the environment can inspire their use that its effect is really felt. Such an atmosphere does not just happen: it has to be planned and worked for and given time to become established. And then it has to be worked at constantly to keep it so. Although finally the atmosphere of a room could be explained by the variety of activities going on, the resourcefulness and imagination, the discoveries made, these did not come about of their own accord. Behind them is a teacher who has made them possible. His influence can be traced everywhere: in the layout of the room; the smooth running of the groups; the use of the room for other occasions; corners where an interest is building up – a puppet theatre under construction, a local excavation being recorded. But above all, the teacher's influence is felt in a manner which is not so obvious or easily explained: it lies in the attitude to work that he has been able to encourage among his classes. The class situation is not a natural one: it is contrived. And no common purpose could form and survive for long without a quiet authority behind it. In any group, spirits are ready for anything: mischief, apathy, serious intention, wit, assault – they are all there. It is the teacher who brings his classes to the threshold of imaginative and practical adventure, and helps them discover that somehow it is important for them: and more than important – enjoyable.

Much of the teacher's inspiration will come from his creativeness as a person: but equally it comes from a concern for his students to find their own, and from his ability to share it with them. Their response to his enthusiasm and his interest in them brings the relationship to life, and continues to renew it day by day as the patterns of response and the individuals change. Like any good workshop, the art room is an organized event. The teacher ensures that students recognize the freedoms and responsibilities they have.

Working arrangements

A variety of processes will be going on in the room, often at the same time. The teacher can plan for this by equipping parts of the room for different activities: a clay area, a carving area, a printmaking area and so on. The flooring, benches and storage should be suitable for these, and any apparatus installed in the best place.

Floors reserved for work with clay or similar materials should be easy to clean and laid with a good quality cork linoleum or vinyl floor covering, or put down as tiles or concrete. Any wood floor is usually better for being sealed. Woodblock flooring has been known to lift in places with too much damping.

If separate areas are not a permanent feature, the teacher will have to set them up whenever necessary by moving furniture and equipment around. He may want to keep certain processes apart, e.g. wet and dry (see page 35). If the benches are fixed, he must arrange for the best use to be made of the places, and improvise any extra ones needed: many purpose-built rooms were not meant for the numbers they now have to accommodate. Otherwise, trestles, tables or desks can be moved around to suit the activity, leaving room to fetch and return materials without upsetting neighbours. The customary arrangement of tables in rows may be satisfactory, but the occasion may call for a different one, e.g. an open square or circle, or smaller groupings within the main one. A very adaptable unit is the trestle table (a solid flat top on folding or fixed trestles). This is strong, has a large surface, and is easily set up and taken down by two students. For a larger working surface, a number of trestle tables can be brought together. The trestles on their own can be used as easels, and the tops as platforms or display boards. Such trestle tables may not be firm enough for heavier jobs like wedging clay or large-scale carving, and these will need special benches or a few robust kitchen tables, usually picked up quite cheaply second-hand.

Stools that tuck away under benches are better than chairs, which are for ever getting in the way. They also serve as additional supports for many kinds of work. A number of radial or smaller easels will be found useful.

Central to all working arrangements is the sink. Experienced teachers know only too well the joys of a really large, well-sited sink. In most cases it is far too small and in the wrong place. It should be possible for several students to be at the sink together, and wash even the biggest bowls and buckets without any problem and with facilities for draining and drying. A sediment trap prevents the soak-away from clogging with thicker waste, though most of this can be kept out of the sink in the first place by cleaning out plaster and other mess into separate bins (different ones for wet and dry rubbish). The wall around the sink should be washable.

It may be felt that the best kind of walls in an art room are bare ones (see page 133), but if the teacher is going to use them for display, he should arrange for as much of them as possible to be faced with a suitable pin-boarding up to a convenient height. The boarding can be glued on or fixed with wall plugs, and then given a coat of flat paint or covered with hessian (burlap) which does not show pin marks.

Lighting

An important consideration in planning work areas is the source of lighting in the room, both from windows and inside fittings. Perhaps the teacher is in a position to influence any installations. All students should be able to work in good light of one kind or the other, and this will affect the arrangement of places. Fluorescent strips that give overall illumination are better than bowl lights that have a restricted range and cast strong shadow, unless they overlap to avoid this. Overhead or wall mountings should be at the right height. Special attention should be paid to parts of the room receiving insufficient light from outside, and switches should control the banks of lights that cover these areas, e.g. parallel to the windows rather than at right-angles to them.

Storage and distribution

The position of shelves, cupboards, drawer chests, drying cabinets and standing bins is vital to the smooth running of the room. Built-in units make better use of space than other kinds. These units may already be installed, but additional ones can be made up to fit recesses. Slatted shelving is satisfactory in many cases: for general purposes though, chipboard or good plywood is more practicable. Cupboards should have sliding doors where possible, and shelves that can be adjusted to different heights. Drawers can be too deep (they get overloaded and difficult to pull out). Drying cabinets and clay bins should be sited near their respective crafts.

Free-standing furniture will probably be required as well, since courses tend to expand and call for ever more storage. A good-sized plan chest will take up to the largest flat material in normal use. Older pieces of furniture with compartments or drawers, again quite reasonably obtained second-hand, are suitable for a variety of storage needs, and often repay the space they take up. Out-of-the-way wall areas and ceilings may solve the problem of hanging materials such as wire coils, cane, laths, battens and lengths of dowelling.

Materials should be stored so that they can be selected and returned easily and without spoiling, especially if students are free to help themselves. For example, a quantity of different coloured craft papers stored flat on top of each other should be light enough in weight for a sheet to be drawn out without a struggle and the risk of tearing it. With cardboard on the other hand, this problem need not arise: the sheets can be stored upright in racks and it is then very simple to lift one out.

Powder or poster colour palettes, stacked to a safe height and contained in some way, will not tip and spill. Having them near their refill containers saves unnecessary carrying and upsets. Brush holders can be obtained or drilled to take the different sized handles. It is helpful to colour the ends of handles and their respective holders with a matching house paint, which makes it easier to return them – and more fun.

A range of adhesives, separated according to their main purposes, reduces waste and misuse. (See Adhesive Tables in *Creative Crafts for Today*, Studio Vista.) Specialist and scrap materials need to be in clearly marked containers. These include covered bins for wet materials like clay, or dry bulk materials like plaster. Heavily loaded containers should be accessible without having to be pulled right out each time. Rigid length-materials like laths or wire rods should be housed in a way that allows one or more to be withdrawn without toppling the rest or causing damage with their ends.

Tools should also be stored neatly in compartments or racks according to their chief uses. Peg-board mounted upright displays most tools well. There are clips for using with this, and an outline drawing of each tool round its clip helps to ensure that it is put back correctly. Little mention need be made of the extra care required with cutting tools, both as regards safety and the protection of edges.

The arrangements for distribution will depend on the size and nature of the class. Some teachers prefer to have it done by monitors, others like each student to see to his own. The smaller and more responsible the class, the more freedom the teacher will feel he can allow. Whatever happens, he should keep an eye on things generally to make sure that everybody has what is required and that responsibilities for items are not confused. Tools and apparatus must be looked after and maintained in good working condition. Students can help with this, spending time every so often checking them over for parts working loose, edges thickening and so on.

Apart from day-to-day needs, the teacher also has to find room for the stock he holds in reserve. He may have somewhere put aside for this, or have to make do with a corner of the art room. Either way, he should organize his stock so that he can bring it into use when needed and, at the same time, keep watch on what he will have to re-order. Only the firmest understanding with his classes will prevent this stock getting into circulation 'by accident'!

Now, where to store the work itself? This can become a problem, especially when a great variety is being produced. Much can be done in ways discussed above, remembering that there will be both finished pieces and those still being worked on. Also, sets from different groups, often from individuals, will have to be kept separate. Flat work is not much trouble: a plan chest as above, shelf space, or stout folders may be all that is needed. Three-dimensional pieces are not so easily 'filed away': shelves, cupboards, and even hanging space quickly fill up; and letting work pile up under tables or in odd corners means that it is always getting in the way or gathering dust. It would be better to distribute suitable works in other parts of the school and grounds, or even in other centres nearby (see page 135). Because it is not such a simple business to write a name on three-dimensional work as it is on a painting, it is often not done at all – with troublesome consequences. Each piece should bear some means of identification – a mark, a tag, a gummed label.

Increasing numbers of schools, especially the larger ones, are developing specialist departments within the main art area, with rooms equipped for particular crafts such as pottery and print-making. These are generally in the charge of specialist teachers. Much of what has been said above will apply in general terms to such rooms, though each teacher will organize his own for the kind of work being done there. Students will usually spend part of their time in each department to gain experience in the different crafts, and an important consideration arises with regard to integrating these experiences so that they are all felt to contribute to the student's broader creative growth. This, the staff concerned must work out between them.

Ordering supplies

Some Local Education Authorities in England have a central supplies system from which schools order stock. If the teacher can order from where he likes, he should go to the firm who can supply what he wants on the best terms. Prices vary, and it is worth looking around before placing the order. He may order with short or long term economies in mind: for example, a bulk order will probably be cheaper than ordering in small quantities, but can he store a large amount? Some tools are cheap, but will they soon wear out and have to be replaced? Materials or tools from specialist firms cost less sometimes than from general suppliers, though this has to be weighed against any discounts allowed and the convenience of ordering from a single source. Delivery times also vary. Some firms deliver within the week, others take much longer. It is as well to

131

know this beforehand so that goods can be ordered to arrive when they are wanted – not too late, and not too soon: storage may again be a problem.

There is no doubt that, by studying the various catalogues and knowing his district, the teacher can make real economies. A pottery or tile works in his area may be able to supply clay cheaper than main suppliers; and if he can arrange for its collection, he can save freight charges – often a big part of the overall cost. Enquiries round about will nearly always come up with some local source of materials, possibly to be had at no cost at all: reel-ends of newsprint, cartons and out-of-date display boards, polystyrene (U.S. styrofoam) packing, reject tiles suitable for breaking up for mosaics, fabric remnants, machine trimmings, hardboard off-cuts and so on.

Saving of a different kind can be made by improvising materials and tools, e.g. colours from natural sources, handmade squeegees or modelling tools. But more important than the saving in this case, is the added significance the work has when the student is using things he makes himself, especially if he has had to design them for a particular purpose. Apart from which, many such tools are a stimulus in themselves, e.g. homemade paint spreaders lead to paintings that would never have come from a brush. The allowance for materials and tools should be watched carefully until the pattern of work for the year has taken shape. It is usually advisable to spread spending over the three terms. A small reserve kept in hand will meet the inevitable call for extras as the courses develop.

Apparatus and equipment
The teacher will also want to equip the room with essential apparatus such as a good-sized guillotine (U.S. paper-cutter) with guard, a press, a staple gun and a range of audio-visual aids. Among those he may find useful are: projectors (16 mm sound cine (U.S. film), 8 mm silent cine, 35 mm filmstrip, 35 mm slide, overhead); tape recorder and spare tapes; tape/slide synchronizer; epidiascope; projector and rear projection screens; cameras (35 mm instamatic, 8 mm cine); record player; typewriter; duplicator; thermo-copier; magnetic board; flock (U.K. flannelgraph) board; self-illuminating microscopes and magnifying lenses. In most schools, equipment of this kind would normally be shared among the various departments, and the art teacher would have to reserve it if he wanted it for a particular lesson. But if he has continual use for a certain item, it would be as well for him to buy it from one of his allowances.

9   Display – do we need it?

There are three opinions about display in the art room:
1 Do;
2 Don't;
3 Do it sometimes.
Any final decision must lie with the teacher, as he sees the needs of the students, the nature of the courses, and the space available. But what support do the opinions have in general terms?

1 Display can give a live, up-to-the-minute picture of the various kinds of work being done throughout the classes. For most students – and staff, come to that – this is the only way of knowing what these are. It reflects the many outlooks, ideas and techniques that are abroad, and makes for greater sharing and understanding. The students are encouraged by seeing their work well mounted and a talking-point among others. Every student can have work up from time to time, for there will always be something he has done a little better than he did before.

2 The best walls are bare walls: display inhibits. The student should be free to develop his own ideas and approach without other examples continually getting in the way. If he sees them, they affect him: if he does not (and few really do), why bother?! Selection of work can lead to invidious comparisons: it sets up a 'teacher likes it' attitude – do it this way and it will be all right. Some students do not like their work seen: it may seem an advance to the teacher but still a poor thing to them. Any large wall space is better used for working on. There will be work around all the time, especially three-dimensional work, some stored openly. This itself is enough to indicate what is going on.

3 Display can usefully show work that sets out to explore different attitudes or aspects: the display in fig. 115, for example, compares the shapes discovered by arranging chairs in various ways. Display can mount a theme running over a period, e.g. people seen from week to week in the district. It can carry a single group work, e.g. a frieze or construction being resumed each time the class returns. From time to time it can rescue work from the oblivion of folders and cupboards and let it see the light of day. There are highlights in the school calendar that work can celebrate in display form, e.g. sports day, an excursion, a festival.

If it is decided that the walls are to be left bare, then their appearance will need thinking about. Should they be painted? If so, what colours would best suit the light conditions and working atmosphere of the room? The parts of the wall lower down should be washable. If the walls are attractive in their natural state, they can be left as they are. If, on the other hand, the walls are to be used for display, what are some of the points to bear in mind?

Fig. 115 Display with a theme. Boys/girls aged 16

The walls should be suitably prepared (see page 128). Work should be mounted well, in reasonable light – sometimes even a directed one, and at a height where it can be easily put up and taken down; work that is difficult to dismantle has a habit of staying up too long. It should be away from likely damage, splashing, or from a source of heat that would cause it to curl. The overall effect may be important: grouping and balance of pieces – a few strong ones can balance a lot of lighter-weight ones or give focus to a broad spread of small work. Any lettering should be clear, simple, and in keeping with the display as a whole.

Students should take part in arranging displays whenever possible. The teacher may make a first selection, but the students should help with the final choice and decide on the setting: coloured or textured backing, mounts, lighting, different level supports for three-dimensional work. Staples or dressmakers' pins are less conspicuous than thumb tacks. Displays should change frequently, and certainly before they have become a fixture that no one notices any more. Some may be seasonal, e.g. for the celebration of a religious festival, and be up for just that time.

Where wall space is inadequate, it might be possible to make up screens supported between uprights, or hinged to stand on their own. Unit screen systems with slotted steel framing can also be obtained, and the units assembled at different angles. Other parts of the room can be used, e.g. windows for work in transparent materials such as glass, cellophane, tissues and gelatines.

Whether or not display is a feature of the art room, there are other places where it can be enjoyed: other parts of the school and grounds (lots of dull flat wall and roof areas could happily take a work); places outside the school, e.g. community centres, club halls, hospitals, old folks' homes (often glad to have such additions). It is good that pieces should get out and about if they give pleasure to others and encouragement to the student. Much work, especially large-scale group work, can in fact be designed for siting outside the room, and even made on the site itself. The concrete horse seen in fig. 116 was carried out in the school grounds, following a small successful pottery model the student had made.

Apart from the students' own work, the teacher may wish to display inspirational material in a central place or in a particular craft area. This might include examples of other art and crafts, or illustrations and information about them. For example, in support of a current weaving project, he might put up actual examples of the cottage weaving industry, pictures of the spinning wheels, looms and dyeing processes, and lengths of natural fleece and yarns. Material of this sort can be acquired outright or on loan from a variety of sources: a schools' circulating scheme, a museum loan service, a local art college, a craft centre or studio workshop, a local industry, a private exchange arrangement with another school, the students themselves (they often travel widely or have interesting things at home that their families would lend). Good mounted sheets take time to prepare: it is worth storing them carefully for possible future use.

10　Visits out of school

The student comes to the art room from a world outside and returns to it afterwards. He can tend to regard the room as somewhere apart from normal everyday life – which it is up to a point, but no more so than the playground or a cinema. Nevertheless, what he does in the room becomes associated with it: it can seem like a pocket of isolated experience. Sometimes it helps if the lesson is taken out of the school altogether. Working trips in connection with art history studies have already been mentioned (page 96). These have a definite end in view; but there is a case for visits whose only point is to be out together, enjoying some place or glimpse into another kind of world. It may be enough for the students that it is in 'art time' for them to be aware of things they would otherwise have missed. But talking among themselves and with the teacher will often focus on something that comes to light, bringing it to mind later in future work. There is no need to make heavy-going of a visit. The lightest direction and a word or two here and there can quicken a reaction and start thoughts moving. In fact, little of value is gained from a trip burdened with obligations to look for this and that, and under the threat of being used in some way on return to school.

Fig. 116 Boy aged 15

Other trips might have a more general aim, e.g. to the country or shore, or to a park or wasteground to collect what can be found; it may be to another school to see what they are doing. But with or without a definite purpose, a visit has to be planned, especially if the group is large or the destination far-off. A few points that the teacher should check are, how many students will there be in the party? Will I need help with the supervision? What arrangements have to be made for the journey: times of leaving and returning, route and costs, dress to be worn, provision of meals, apparatus needed? Is any outside permission required for the visit? Students should be quite clear about arrangements, including possible emergencies. A visit out of school hours may have to make further plans to cover meeting points, separate fares, collection of things from the school, etc. Parents' consent may also be required. If visits are tied in more closely with the students' work, it is useful to have some means of keeping records or collections safe and tidy: individual workbooks, folders or containers. These can become 'tools' of personal investigation, valuable in themselves and the way they are kept, and as a source of ideas. Any collected materials left over can go into the general art room reserves.

The success of any excursion depends on the preparation put into it, the interests it arouses, and the pleasure it gives. Results may not show for a while. But a happy visit will always be remembered by someone.

J

Further reading

General

The nature of creative activity   V. Lowenfeld   ROUTLEDGE & KEGAN PAUL, LONDON.
Creative and mental growth   V. Lowenfeld   COLLIER MACMILLAN, LONDON.
Your child and his art   V. Lowenfeld   COLLIER MACMILLAN, LONDON AND NEW YORK.
Rosegarden and labyrinth   S. Robertson   ROUTLEDGE & KEGAN PAUL, LONDON AND NEW YORK.
Education through art   H. Read   FABER & FABER, LONDON.
Scribbling, drawing, painting   W. Grözinger   FABER & FABER, LONDON.
Art in American life and education   T. Munro   UNIVERSITY OF CHICAGO PRESS.
Arts of man   E. Newton   THAMES & HUDSON, LONDON/N.Y. GRAPHIC SOC., GREENWICH, CONN.
Man the artist – his creative imagination   Ed. Barry/Fisher/Bronowski/Huxley   MACDONALD, LONDON.
The meaning and magic of art   F. Gettings   HAMLYN, LONDON.
Feeling and form   S. Langer   ROUTLEDGE & KEGAN PAUL, LONDON.
The forms of things unknown   H. Read   FABER & FABER, LONDON/MERIDIAN, N.Y.
Art and illusion   E. Gombrich   PHAIDON, LONDON/PRINCETON U. PRESS, PRINCETON, N.J.
Philosophy in a new key   S. Langer   HARVARD UNIVERSITY PRESS/OXFORD UNIVERSITY PRESS, LONDON.
The meaning of art   H. Read   PENGUIN, LONDON/PITMAN, N.Y.
Icon and idea   H. Read   FABER & FABER, LONDON/SCHOCKEN, N.Y.
Seeing and knowing   B. Berenson   EVELYN, LONDON/N.Y. GRAPHIC SOC., GREENWICH, CONN.
Art and visual perception   R. Arnheim   FABER & FABER, LONDON/U. OF CAL. PRESS, BERKELEY, CALIF.
Meditations on a hobby horse   E. Gombrich   PHAIDON, LONDON/PRAEGER, N.Y.
You are an artist   F. Gettings   HAMLYN, LONDON.
Pedagogical sketchbook   P. Klee   FABER & FABER, LONDON/PRAEGER, N.Y.
Van Gogh – letters   Ed. Roskill   FONTANA, LONDON.
Leonardo da Vinci – selections from his notebooks   Ed. Richter   OXFORD UNIVERSITY PRESS, LONDON.
The lives of the artists: Vasari   Transl. G. Bull   PENGUIN, LONDON/FARRAR, STRAUS AND GIROUX, N.Y.

Craft processes

COLLAGE
Collage   F. Brow   PITMAN, LONDON/GROSSET AND DUNLAP, N.Y.
Creating in collage   N. d'Arbeloff/J. Yates   STUDIO VISTA, LONDON/WATSON-GUPTILL, N.Y.
Collage and found art   D. Meilach   VAN NOSTRAND REINHOLD, N.Y.

DRAWING AND PAINTING
Creative drawing – point and line   E. Röttger   BATSFORD, LONDON/VAN NOSTRAND REINHOLD, N.Y.
Creative pencil drawing   P. Hogarth   STUDIO VISTA, LONDON/WATSON-GUPTILL, N.Y.
Exploring with paint   Petterson/Gerring   STUDIO VISTA, LONDON/VAN NOSTRAND REINHOLD, N.Y.
Materials of the artist   M. Doerner   HART DAVIS, LONDON/HARCOURT BRACE, N.Y.
Painter's pocket book   H. Hiler   FABER & FABER, LONDON/WATSON-GUPTILL, N.Y.
An artist's workbook   N. d'Arbeloff   STUDIO VISTA, LONDON/VAN NOSTRAND REINHOLD, N.Y.
Drawing with pencil   Laliberte/Mogelon   VAN NOSTRAND REINHOLD, N.Y.
Drawing with ink   Laliberte/Mogelon   VAN NOSTRAND REINHOLD, N.Y.

EMBROIDERY AND FABRIC CRAFT
Teaching children embroidery   A. Butler   STUDIO VISTA, LONDON

Stitches of creative embroidery J. Enthoven VAN NOSTRAND REINHOLD, N.Y.
Inspiration for embroidery C. Howard BATSFORD, LONDON/BRANFORD, NEWTON CENTRE, MASS.
Curve stitching (Mathematical topics, 2nd Year, Book 2) E. James OXFORD UNIVERSITY PRESS, LONDON.
Fabric printing by hand S. Russ STUDIO VISTA, LONDON/WATSON-GUPTILL, N.Y.
Colour and texture in creative textile craft (U.S. Creative Textile Design) R. Hartung BATSFORD, LONDON/VAN NOSTRAND REINHOLD, N.Y.
Batik: art and craft N. Krevitsky VAN NOSTRAND REINHOLD, N.Y.
Stitchery: art and craft N. Krevitsky VAN NOSTRAND REINHOLD, N.Y.
Design on Fabric Johnston/Kaufman VAN NOSTRAND REINHOLD, N.Y.
Weaving is for anyone J. Wilson STUDIO VISTA, LONDON/VAN NOSTRAND REINHOLD, N.Y.
Tie-and-dye as a present day craft A. Maile MILLS & BOON, LONDON/TAPLINGER, N.Y.
Fabric pictures E. Alexander MILLS & BOON, LONDON/HEARTHSIDE, N.Y.
The weaver's craft Simpson/Weir DRYAD, LONDON.

LETTERING
Lettering H. Degering BENN, LONDON.
Lettering C. R. Anderson VAN NOSTRAND REINHOLD, N.Y.
Anatomy of lettering R. Laker STUDIO VISTA, LONDON/VIKING PRESS, N.Y.
Writing and illuminating and lettering E. Johnston PITMAN, LONDON.

MOSAICS
Making mosaics J. Berry STUDIO VISTA, LONDON/WATSON-GUPTILL, N.Y.
Mosaic making H. Hutton BATSFORD, LONDON/VAN NOSTRAND REINHOLD, N.Y.
Pottery and mosaics H. Powell BLANDFORD, LONDON/BRANFORD, NEWTON CENTRE, MASS.

PAPER CRAFT
Creative paper craft (U.S. Creative paper design) E. Röttger BATSFORD, LONDON/VAN NOSTRAND REINHOLD, N.Y.
Creating with paper P. Johnson KAYE, LONDON/UNIVERSITY OF WASHINGTON PRESS, SEATTLE, WASH.
Origami – birds, flowers, animals, fishes METHUEN, LONDON.
Creative corrugated paper craft (U.S. Creating with corrugated paper) R. Hartung BATSFORD, LONDON/VAN NOSTRAND REINHOLD, N.Y.

POTTERY
Simple pottery K. Drake STUDIO VISTA, LONDON/WATSON-GUPTILL, N.Y.
Technique of pottery D. Billington BATSFORD, LONDON/HEARTHSIDE, N.Y.
Potter's book B. Leach FABER & FABER, LONDON/TRANSATLANTIC, N.Y.
Clay and glazes for the potter D. Rhodes PITMAN, LONDON/CHILTON BOOK CO, PHILADELPHIA, PA.
Making pottery without a wheel Ball/Lovoos VAN NOSTRAND REINHOLD, N.Y.
Creating form in clay Petterson VAN NOSTRAND REINHOLD, N.Y.

PRINTMAKING
Creative printmaking P. Green BATSFORD, LONDON/WATSON-GUPTILL, N.Y.
Young printmaker H. Weiss KAYE, LONDON/WM. R. SCOTT, N.Y.
Frontiers of printmaking M. Rothenstein STUDIO VISTA, LONDON/VAN NOSTRAND REINHOLD, N.Y.
Lino cuts and wood cuts M. Rothenstein STUDIO VISTA, LONDON/WATSON-GUPTILL, N.Y.
Printingmaking without a press Erickson/Sproul VAN NOSTRAND REINHOLD, N.Y.
The technique of fine art lithography Knigin/Zimiles VAN NOSTRAND REINHOLD, N.Y.
Screen process printing J. and M. Schwalbach VAN NOSTRAND REINHOLD, N.Y.
Rubbings and textures J. Bodor VAN NOSTRAND REINHOLD, N.Y.

PUPPETRY
Puppet book Ed. Philpott/Wall/White FABER & FABER, LONDON/PLAYS, BOSTON, MASS.
You can make a string puppet R. Slade FABER & FABER, LONDON/PLAYS, BOSTON, MASS.
Shadow puppets O. Blackham BARRIE & ROCKLIFF, LONDON.
Puppetry today H. Binyon STUDIO VISTA, LONDON.
The book of puppetry Bufano COLLIER MACMILLAN, LONDON.

SCULPTURE AND MODELLING
Wood carving A. Durst STUDIO VISTA, LONDON/VIKING, N.Y.
Creative wood craft (U.S. *Creative wood design*) E. Röttger BATSFORD, LONDON/
VAN NOSTRAND REINHOLD, N.Y.
Whittling and wood carving B. Tangerman DOVER, LONDON AND N.Y.
The young sculptor H. Weiss KAYE, LONDON/WM. R. SCOTT, N.Y.
Materials and methods of sculpture J. Rich OXFORD UNIVERSITY PRESS, LONDON
AND N.Y.
Art of sculpture H. Read FABER & FABER, LONDON/PRINCETON U. PRESS, N.J.
New materials in sculpture H. Percy TIRANTI, LONDON/TRANSATLANTIC, LEVIT-
TOWN, L.I., N.Y.
Creative clay craft E. Röttger BATSFORD, LONDON/VAN NOSTRAND REINHOLD, N.Y.
Direct metal sculpture Meilach/Seiden ALLEN & UNWIN, LONDON/CROWN, N.Y.
Making mobiles A. & C. Moorey STUDIO VISTA, LONDON/WATSON-GUPTILL, N.Y.
Decorative straw work Davis/Sandford BATSFORD, LONDON.
Creative crafts for today J. Portchmouth STUDIO VISTA, LONDON/VIKING, N.Y.
Fantasy furniture Simpson VAN NOSTRAND REINHOLD, N.Y.

Other curriculum subjects

DOMESTIC AND PRACTICAL CRAFT AREAS
The story of your home A. Allen FABER & FABER, LONDON/TRANSATLANTIC,
LEVITTOWN, L.I., N.Y.
Homes in Great Britain A. Barfoot BATSFORD, LONDON/DUFOUR EDITIONS, CHESTER
SPRINGS, P.A.
The golden age of homespun J. van Wagenen CORNELL UNIVERSITY PRESS, N.Y.
Here of all places O. Lancaster MURRAY, LONDON/HOUGHTON MIFFLIN, BOSTON.
English costume I. Brooke BLACK, LONDON/BARNES AND NOBLE, N.Y.
Costume through the ages J. Laver THAMES & HUDSON, LONDON/SIMON & SCHUSTER,
N.Y.
Popular art in England G. Fletcher HARRAP, LONDON.
Country crafts and craftsmen G. Hogg HUTCHINSON, LONDON.
Man the tool maker K. Oakley BRITISH MUSEUM, LONDON/UNIV. OF CHICAGO PRESS,
CHICAGO.
Creative crafts in education S. Robertson. ROUTLEDGE & KEGAN PAUL, LONDON.
Basic design M. de Sausmarez STUDIO VISTA, LONDON/VAN NOSTRAND REINHOLD,
N.Y.
The nature of design D. Pye STUDIO VISTA, LONDON/VAN NOSTRAND REINHOLD, N.Y.
Wood specimens Ed. P. Nairn TOTHILL PRESS, LONDON.
Rural costume Oakes/Hill VAN NOSTRAND REINHOLD, N.Y.
The evolution of fashion Hill/Bucknell VAN NOSTRAND REINHOLD, N.Y.

DRAMA
The empty space P. Brook MACGIBBON & KEE, LONDON/AVON, N.Y.
Child drama P. Slade UNIVERSITY OF LONDON PRESS/VERRY, LAWRENCE, MYSTIC,
CONN.
Shakespeare and the actors I. Brown BODLEY HEAD, LONDON/COWARD-MCCANN
INC., N.Y.
Directing a play J. Roose-Evans STUDIO VISTA, LONDON/THEATRE ARTS, N.Y.
Designing and making stage scenery M. Warre STUDIO VISTA, LONDON/VAN
NOSTRAND REINHOLD, N.Y.
Simple stage costumes S. Jackson STUDIO VISTA, LONDON/WATSON-GUPTILL, N.Y.
Designing and making stage costumes 'Motley' STUDIO VISTA, LONDON/WATSON-
GUPTILL, N.Y.
Film makers on film making Ed. H. Geduld PENGUIN, LONDON/INDIANA UNIVER-
SITY PRESS, BLOOMINGTON, IND.
Dictionary of the theatre PENGUIN, LONDON.
The theatre of the absurd M. Esslin PENGUIN, LONDON/DOUBLEDAY, N.Y.
History of the English puppet theatre G. Speaight HARRAP, LONDON/PLAYS, INC.,
BOSTON, MASS.
Chinese puppet theatre S. Obratzov FABER & FABER, LONDON/PLAYS, INC., BOSTON,
MASS.
Punch and Judy Fraser VAN NOSTRAND REINHOLD, N.Y.
Film making in the schools J. Lidstone VAN NOSTRAND REINHOLD, N.Y.
Play with light and shadow H. Schonewolf STUDIO VISTA, LONDON/VAN NOSTRAND
REINHOLD, N.Y.
Presenting Marionnettes S. French VAN NOSTRAND REINHOLD, N.Y.

140

GEOGRAPHY
Earth in upheaval   I. Velikovsky   GOLLANCZ, LONDON/DOUBLEDAY, N.Y.
Worlds in collision   I. Velikovsky   GOLLANCZ, LONDON/DOUBLEDAY, N.Y.
The earth   N. Harris and others   HAMLYN, LONDON/OUTLET, N.Y.
A land   J. Hawkes   PENGUIN, LONDON/DUFOUR, CHESTER SPRINGS, PA.
Beyond time   M. Siffre   CHATTO & WINDUS, LONDON/MCGRAW-HILL, N.Y.
Potholing: Beneath the Northern Pennines   D. Heap   ROUTLEDGE & KEGAN PAUL, LONDON.
The ways of the sea   R. Pilkington   ROUTLEDGE & KEGAN PAUL, LONDON.
The sea around us   R. Carson   STAPLES, LONDON/WESTERN PUB. CO., RACINE, WIS.
The elements rage   F. Lane   DAVID & CHARLES, LONDON/CHILTON, PHILADELPHIA, PA.
Clouds and weather   R. Pilsbury   BATSFORD, LONDON.
The Kon-Tiki expedition   T. Heyerdahl   PENGUIN, LONDON/RAND MCNALLY, N.Y.
The travels of Marco Polo   PENGUIN, LONDON.
The lost world of the Kalahari   L. Van der Post   PENGUIN, LONDON/APOLLO, N.Y.
Folk art of Europe   H. Bossert   ZWEMMER, LONDON/PRAEGER, N.Y.
Folk art of primitive peoples   H. Bossert   ZWEMMER, LONDON/PRAEGER, N.Y.

HISTORY AND SOCIAL STUDIES
The Penguin book of lost worlds   L. Cottrell   PENGUIN, LONDON/AMERICAN HERITAGE PUBLISHING, N.Y.
Exploring the past, Books I–III   Wright/Hanson/Bridges   CASSELL, LONDON.
Digging up the past   L. Woolley   PENGUIN, LONDON AND BALTIMORE.
The Sutton Hoo ship burial   R. Mitford   BRITISH MUSEUM, LONDON.
Heraldry   C. Boutell   FREDERICK WARNE, LONDON AND N.Y.
Pageant of heraldry   H. Rogers   SEELEY, LONDON.
Arms and armour   A. Norman   WEIDENFELD & NICOLSON, LONDON/PUTNAM'S, N.Y.
Brass rubbing   M. Norris   STUDIO VISTA, LONDON.
The Bayeux tapestry   Denny/Sankey   COLLINS, LONDON/ANTHENEUM PUBLISHERS, N.Y.
Decorative arts of the mariner   Ed. G. Frere-Cook   CASSELL, LONDON/LITTLE, BROWN, BOSTON.
English merchants' marks   F. Girling   OXFORD UNIVERSITY PRESS, LONDON AND NEW YORK.
Medieval manuscript painting   S. Mitchell   WEIDENFELD & NICOLSON, LONDON/ VIKING PRESS, N.Y.
Costume cavalcade   H. Hansen   METHUEN, LONDON.
1066 and all that   Sellar/Yeatman   PENGUIN, LONDON/DUTTON, N.Y.
Illustrated English social history   G. Trevelyan   PENGUIN, LONDON/MCKAY, N.Y.
Hogarth to Cruickshank – Social change in graphic satire   M. George   PENGUIN, LONDON/WALKER AND CO., N.Y.
The rise of the meritocracy   M. Young   PENGUIN, LONDON AND BALTIMORE.
The hidden persuaders   V. Packard   PENGUIN, LONDON/SIMON & SCHUSTER, N.Y.
The waste makers   V. Packard   PENGUIN, LONDON/SIMON & SCHUSTER, N.Y.
The death and life of great American cities   J. Jacobs   PENGUIN, LONDON/RANDOM HOUSE INC., N.Y.
The American city: a source book of urban imagery   Ed. A. Strauss   PENGUIN, LONDON/ALDINE BOOKS, N.Y.
Traffic in towns   Buchanan report   PENGUIN, LONDON/BRITISH INFORMATION SERVICES, N.Y.
From the cave to the city   P. Lynch   ARNOLD, LONDON/ST. MARTIN'S PRESS, INC., N.Y.
World Architecture   Ed. T. Copplestone   HAMLYN, LONDON/OUTLET, N.Y.

LANGUAGE
Studies in words   C. S. Lewis   CAMBRIDGE UNIVERSITY PRESS, LONDON AND NEW YORK.
You English words   J. Moore   COLLINS, LONDON/LIPPINCOTT, PHILADELPHIA.
Naming-day in Eden   N. Jacobs   GOLLANCZ, LONDON/MACMILLAN, N.Y.
The man who could read stones   A. Honour   WORLD'S WORK, LONDON/HAWTHORN, N.Y.
Forgotten scripts   C. Gordon   THAMES & HUDSON, LONDON/BASIC BOOKS INC., N.Y.
Writing   D. Diringer   THAMES & HUDSON, LONDON/PRAEGER, N.Y.
The lore and language of schoolchildren   I. & P. Opie   OXFORD UNIVERSITY PRESS, LONDON AND NEW YORK.
Miracles – poems by children of the English speaking world   Ed. R. Lewis   PENGUIN, LONDON/SIMON & SCHUSTER, N.Y.
Wild Wales   G. Borrow   COLLINS, LONDON/DUTTON, N.Y.

Early illuminated manuscripts Swarzenski STUDIO VISTA, LONDON.
500 years of printing J. Steinberg PENGUIN, LONDON AND BALTIMORE.
The 26 letters O. Ogg HARRAP, LONDON/THOMAS Y. CROWELL CO., N.Y.
A book of scripts A. Fairbank PENGUIN, LONDON AND BALTIMORE.
Books from papyrus to paperback Harley/Hampden METHUEN, LONDON/ROY PUBLISHERS, N.Y.
The design of books A. Wilson STUDIO VISTA, LONDON/VAN NOSTRAND REINHOLD, N.Y.
Signs in action J. Sutton STUDIO VISTA, LONDON/VAN NOSTRAND REINHOLD, N.Y.
Illustrators at work R. Jacques STUDIO VISTA, LONDON/DUFOUR, CHESTER SPRINGS, PA.
Japanese woodblock prints S. Fijikake JAPANESE TRAVEL BUREAU.

MATHEMATICS
The wonderful world of mathematics L. Hogben MACDONALD, LONDON/DOUBLE-DAY, N.Y.
The language of mathematics F. Land MURRAY, LONDON/DOUBLEDAY, N.Y.
Mathematics in the making L. Hogben MACDONALD, LONDON.
Realm of numbers I. Asimov GOLLANCZ, LONDON/HOUGHTON MIFFLIN, BOSTON.
Maths for those who hate it R. Hartkopf ANGUS & ROBERTSON, LONDON/EMERSON BOOKS, N.Y.
Mathematics on vacation J. Madachy NELSON, LONDON/CHARLES SCRIBNER, N.Y.
Mathematics at the fireside G. Shackle CAMBRIDGE UNIVERSITY PRESS, LONDON.
Discovery of the circle B. Munari TIRANTI, LONDON/GEORGE WITTENBORN, N.Y.
Playing with infinity R. Péter BELL, LONDON/SIMON & SCHUSTER, N.Y.
Understanding the new mathematics E. Rosenthal SOUVENIR PRESS, LONDON/FAWCETT, N.Y.
Thinking machines I. Adler DOBSON, LONDON/JOHN DAY, N.Y.
Mathematics and the imagination Kasner/Newman PENGUIN, LONDON/SIMON & SCHUSTER, N.Y.
Introducing mathematics W. Sawyer PENGUIN, LONDON.

MUSIC
The infinite variety of music L. Bernstein WEIDENFELD & NICOLSON, LONDON/SIMON & SCHUSTER, N.Y.
Music tells the tale Palmer/Lloyd FREDERICK WARNE, LONDON AND N.Y.
The Pelican history of music Ed. Robertson/Stevens PENGUIN, LONDON AND BALTIMORE.
Man through his art, Vol. 2. Music Eds. De Silva/Von Simson EDUCATIONAL PRODUCTIONS, LONDON/NEW YORK GRAPHIC SOC., GREENWICH, CONN.
Opera nights E. Newman PUTNAM, LONDON.
Standard stories from the operas G. Davidson WERNER LAURIE, LONDON.
A concise history of ballet F. Reyna THAMES & HUDSON, LONDON/GROSSET & DUNLAP, N.Y.
All what jazz P. Larkin FABER & FABER, LONDON/ST. MARTIN'S PRESS, N.Y.
Blues people LeRoi Jones MACGIBBON & KEE, LONDON/MORROW, N.Y.
Musical instruments in art and history Bragard/de Hen BARRIE & ROCKLIFF, LONDON/VIKING PRESS, N.Y.
Musical instruments through the ages Ed. A. Baines PENGUIN, LONDON/WALKER & CO., N.Y.
Mozart's letters Ed. E. Blom PENGUIN, LONDON AND NEW YORK.

RELIGIOUS STUDIES
Sacred books of the world A. Bouquet PENGUIN, LONDON/BARNES & NOBLE, N.Y.
Comparative religion A. Bouquet PENGUIN, LONDON AND BALTIMORE.
The Penguin history of Christianity R. Bainton PENGUIN, LONDON/AMERICAN HERITAGE PUBLISHING CO., N.Y.
Signs and symbols in Christian art G. Ferguson OXFORD UNIVERSITY PRESS, LONDON & NEW YORK.
Dictionary of saints PENGUIN, LONDON.
New Larousse encyclopaedia of mythology Intro. R. Graves HAMLYN, LONDON/OUTLET, N.Y.
Greek myths R. Graves PENGUIN, LONDON AND NEW YORK.
Bunyan, The Pilgrim's progress Ed. R. Sharrock PENGUIN, LONDON.
The quest of the Holy Grail Tr. P. M. Matarasso PENGUIN, LONDON AND BALTIMORE.
Homer, Iliad and Odyssey E. Rieu PENGUIN, LONDON.
Dante, The Divine Comedy D. Sayers PENGUIN, LONDON.

Virgil, The Aeneid W. Jackson Knight PENGUIN, LONDON.
Witchcraft and sorcery Ed. M. Marwick PENGUIN, LONDON AND BALTIMORE.
The survival of God in the scientific age A. Isaacs PENGUIN, LONDON AND BALTIMORE.
How to study an old church A. Needham BATSFORD, LONDON.
Phoenix at Coventry B. Spence G. BLES, LONDON/HARPER AND ROW, N.Y.

SCIENCE
The universe: from flat earth to quasar I. Asimov PENGUIN, LONDON.
Environments out there I. Asimov ABELARD-SCHUMAN, LONDON AND NEW YORK.
The sky at night P. Moore EYRE & SPOTTISWOODE, LONDON.
Man's conquest of the stars P. Rousseau JARROLDS, LONDON.
The fabric of the heavens Toulmin/Goodfield PENGUIN, LONDON/HARPER AND ROW, N.Y.
The invasion of the moon P. Ryan PENGUIN, LONDON AND NEW YORK.
The clock we live on I. Asimov ABELARD-SCHUMAN, LONDON AND NEW YORK.
The 365 days K. Irwin HARRAP, LONDON/THOMAS Y. CROWELL, N.Y.
The voices of time Ed. J. Fraser PENGUIN, LONDON/BRAZILLER, N.Y.
Men, ants and elephants P. Weyl PHOENIX HOUSE, LONDON/VIKING PRESS, N.Y.
The senses of animals Matthews/Knight MUSEUM PRESS, LONDON/PHILOSOPHICAL LIBRARY, N.Y.
King Solomon's ring K. Lorenz METHUEN, LONDON/THOMAS Y. CROWELL, N.Y.
Darwin and the 'Beagle' A. Moorehead HAMISH HAMILTON, LONDON/HARPER & ROW, N.Y.
The book of beasts Transl. T. White CAPE, LONDON/G. P. PUTNAM'S SONS, N.Y.
The book of British birds DRIVE PUBLICATIONS, LONDON.
The pictorial encyclopaedia of insects V. J. Stavek HAMLYN, LONDON/CROWN, N.Y.
The pictorial encyclopaedia of the animal kingdom V. J. Stavek HAMLYN, LONDON/CROWN, N.Y.
Abyss C. Idyll CONSTABLE, LONDON/THOMAS Y. CROWELL, N.Y.
Silent Spring R. Carson PENGUIN, LONDON/HOUGHTON MIFFLIN, BOSTON.
The edge of the sea R. Carson PANTHER, LONDON/HOUGHTON MIFFLIN, BOSTON.
New treasury of science Ed. Shapley and others COLLINS, LONDON/HARPER & ROW, N.Y.
Exploring the world of science Obourn and others D. VAN NOSTRAND, LONDON.
Optical illusions and the visual arts Carraher/Thurston STUDIO VISTA, LONDON/VAN NOSTRAND REINHOLD, N.Y.

SPORT
Skill in sport: the attainment of proficiency B. Knapp ROUTLEDGE & KEGAN PAUL, LONDON/SOCCER ASSOCIATES, N.Y.
The spectator's handbook J. Pick PHOENIX SPORTS BOOKS, LONDON.
Children's games in streets and playground I. & P. Opie OXFORD UNIVERSITY PRESS, LONDON AND NEW YORK.
A history of toys A. Fraser WEIDENFELD & NICOLSON, LONDON/DELL, N.Y.

Index